Conflict, Culture, Change

Conflict, Culture, Change

Engaged Buddhism in a

Globalizing World

Sulak Sivaraksa

Wisdom Publications • Boston

Dedications

Respectfully dedicated to Mr. Direk Jayanama
1905–1967
diplomat, statesman, and gentleman

Mr. Kulap Saipradit
1905–1974
novelist, journalist, and gentleman

Rev. Prebendary John A. Rogers
1934–1995
true spiritual friend

Dr. David Chappell
1940–2004
the wisest, the most broad-minded, and the best

Wisdom Publications
199 Elm Street
Somerville, MA 02144 USA
www.wisdompubs.org

Library of Congress Cataloging-in-Publication Data
Sulak Sivaraksa.
  Conflict, culture, change : engaged buddhism in a globalizing world /
Sulak Sivaraksa.—1st ed.
    p. cm.
  Includes bibliographical references.
  ISBN 0-86171–498–9 (pbk. : alk. paper)
  1. Buddhism—Social aspects. 2. Buddhism—Thailand—History—
20th century. I. Title.
  BQ4570.S6S9 2005
  294.3'37—dc22

                                    2004029378
First Edition
09 08 07 06 05
5   4   3   2   1

Cover design by TLrggms

Interior design by Gallery223. Set in Centaur Mt 11/5/15.

Printed in the United States of America.

Contents

Foreword

The Many Faces of Sulak Sivaraksa

IT HAS BEEN MY HONOR and pleasure to know Acharn Sulak for nearly forty years, as a friend, colleague, teacher, and student. He is many things to many people—traditional Thai scholar and global networker, writer and critic, activist and provocateur. There is Sulak-of-the-elite and Sulak-of-the-masses. This book reveals these many facets of a modern traditionalist caught in the belly of a paradox.

Sulak promotes dialogue, reconciliation, and compassion, yet he attacks, with thinly veiled righteous anger, America's global dominance, his own government's harsh treatment of villagers displaced by the Pak Moon dam, and China's disregard for the cultural and ethnic integrity of Tibet. He tilts at the windmills of transnational corporations, while participating in World Bank–sponsored events such as the World Faiths Development Dialogue. He rails against the deleterious consequences of globalization, yet he is cofounder of the global International Network of Engaged Buddhists. And there is the paradox of Sulak's frenetic schedule alongside his appreciation of monastic simplicity, breathing meditation, and a nonmaterialistic lifestyle.

Conflict, Culture, Change includes themes familiar to Sulak's readers: the cultural and environmental impacts of consumerism; understanding, nonviolence, and compassion in the aftermath of 9-11; the integration of mindfulness with social activism; using Buddhist ethics to confront structural violence; and globalization's threat to traditional identity. This book is an informative introduction to his wide range of interests and commitments. It also breaks new ground: a discussion of Buddhist education, insights on interreligious dialogue (see chapters 6 and 8), and analyses of the transformation of Thailand during the past three-quarters of a century.

Since Acharn Sulak taught with me at Swarthmore College last year, his students continue to speak about his breadth of knowledge and experience, and even more so about his openness to them in the classroom and at his home. Although a book cannot substitute for a conversation, these essays introduce the reader to Sulak as a person—his warmth, commitment, and creativity—and invite the reader to come to know one of the founders of the worldwide movement of socially engaged spirituality. *Conflict, Culture, Change* is a welcome addition to the growing literature on contemporary global Buddhism. It is intended to provoke, and I believe it will.

Donald K. Swearer
Director, Center for the Study of World Religions
Harvard Divinity School
February 2004
Chiang Mai, Thailand

Peace, Nonviolence, and Social Justice

1. Buddhist Solutions to Global Conflict

Peacemaking, Peace-Building, and Peacekeeping

WHEN TWO PARTIES LISTEN to each other and see one another not as enemies but as human beings, the animosity between them can be dissolved. So much can be achieved through dialogue. Overcoming dualistic thinking that sees the world as good or evil, friend or foe, is the basis of nonviolence, and nonviolence is the basis of peace.

When Nagarjuna, the great third-century Indian Buddhist scholar, was asked to summarize the Buddha's teaching, he replied, *"Ahimsa,"* nonviolence. Nonviolence is the most basic teaching of the Buddha. There is, however, a misconception that nonviolence is equivalent to inaction. Samdhong Rinpoche, the Prime Minister of the Tibetan Government-in-Exile, says, "Nonviolence is an action, not merely the absence of violence."

Buddha's teachings define violence in great detail. Every action has three doors, he taught, or three ways we create karma: through body, speech, and mind.

He further posited that every action originates in the mind and is then expressed through either speech or a bodily act. For a violent action to occur, there must first be a wish in one's mind to commit the action. This mental violence is of three types: greed, hatred, and delusion or ignorance. Known as the Three Poisons, they are regarded as the root causes of the violence that is subsequently expressed through body and speech. Some people may commit a violent act because of ignorance—not knowing right from wrong. Others may do it out of hatred, or anger.

The Buddha taught his followers that there are four types of verbal violence: divisive speech, gossip, harmful words, and slander, and three types of physical violence: killing, stealing, and sexual misconduct. For an act of violence to occur, he said, there needs to be an object for that act. The person committing the act always carries it out against an object. So to carry out a nonviolent action you need a desire or intention, an object, and the carrying out of the action. An action can be either partially or completely fulfilled.

Because violence has its origins in the Three Poisons of greed, hatred, and ignorance, to act nonviolently we must overcome these poisons. We must develop the opposite mental attitude. The *paramitas*, or transcendental actions, provide the basis for nonviolent action. The Six Paramitas in the Mahayana tradition are generosity, morality, patience, effort, meditation, and wisdom. The Theravada tradition has an additional four—renunciation, truth, resolution, and loving-kindness—and equanimity takes the place of meditation, although meditation is implied if you wish to practice the transcendent action to perfection.

Hence, merely refraining from an act of violence succeeds in overcoming violence only on a basic level. To cultivate good qualities of mind and actively carry out nonviolent actions represents a deeper understanding. So, to truly practice nonviolence we need to transform the Three Poisons of greed, anger, and ignorance and cultivate positive qualities by practicing the Six Paramitas and/or the Four Brahmaviharas, or "Divine Abodes"—*metta, karuna, mudita,* and *upekkha* (loving-kindness, compassion, sympathetic joy, and equanimity).[1]

The practice of meditation is very important. Practicing meditation allows us to understand what controls us, to really know our own mind. We can see the love, hate, fear, and delusion in our minds. By understanding and acknowledging these emotions, we can overcome our prejudices. This provides a basis for problem solving, a basis of wisdom and compassion. Together these can provide the basis for a nonviolent response.

Meditation practice cultivates the development of upekkha, equanimity. The one who has equanimity is fully aware of what is going on without being blinded by attachment, or clinging. This does not mean hermet-like isolation, apathy, or insensitivity. It is a mindful detachment that allows the development of wisdom. Wisdom is what really allows us to help others with compassion and understanding.

The bodhisattva, the person committed to liberation of all others, does not turn away from violence and suffering. The bodhisattva has both the wisdom and compassion to understand and respond to suffering. Again, nonviolence does not mean turning way from violence or being passive. It means responding to violence with *upaya*, or skillful means, action appropriate to the time and circumstance. Let us look at the life of the Buddha for an example of upaya being used to respond to a violent situation.

A conflict had broken out between the Shakyas and the Koliyas over water, and the kings of the two states were preparing to go to war. The Buddha came and said to one of the kings, "How much is water worth, great king?"

"Very little, reverend sir," he replied.

"How much are warriors worth, great king?"

"They are beyond price," he replied.

Then the Buddha said, "It is not fitting that for a little water you should destroy warriors who are beyond price."

Those listening fell silent. The Buddha addressed them, "Great kings, why do you act in this manner? Were I not present today you would set flowing a river of blood. You have acted in a most unbecoming manner."[2]

Had the Buddha done nothing and allowed war to begin, that would not have been nonviolent. Failing to intervene in this situation would have been an act of violence. This illustration shows us that Buddhism is not otherworldly but is actively *engaged* with the world. Unfortunately, many Buddhists are content with their own inner peace and do not relate to the world around them. Burma, for instance, has many great meditation masters; you can go to the temples there and enjoy wonderful meditation practice. But what about outside the temples? The country is a military dictatorship, and there are many terrible abuses of human rights.3 Staying in the temple and meditating is not practicing nonviolence. We need to *engage* with the world.

We should not forget the law of karma: Everything we experience is the result of previous causes and conditions. And everything we do creates future results. As the opening verses of the *Dhammapada* teach us, "If one acts with a corrupt mind, suffering follows. If one acts with a serene mind, peace follows."4 We must be aware that how we act now will affect our life (and the world) in the future. We reap what we sow and cannot avoid the results of our karma. If we have this awareness, we will try our best to sow seeds of peace.

Another story from the life of the Buddha demonstrates the law of karma. The King of Kosala wanted to be related to the Buddha, so he asked for a princess from the royal Shakya family to be his queen. The Shakya clan, into which the Buddha was born, was very caste-conscious and refused to allow the marriage. Although they regarded Kosala as a mighty kingdom, they did not regard that family's caste as equal to theirs. So, instead of sending the King of Kosala a princess, they sent him the daughter of a slave woman. As Queen of Kosala, she gave birth to a prince named Vidhudhabha. Nobody in Kosala knew that their Queen was an outcaste slave girl. But when the young prince went to visit his maternal grandfather and his other Shakya relatives, he discovered that the Shakyans looked down on him because his mother was a slave. So the young prince vowed to kill all members of the Shakya clan in revenge.

When Vidhudhabha succeeded his father to the throne of Kosala, he marched his army northward. The Buddha knew of the situation and went to sit at the border of the two kingdoms, and on three occasions he was able to stop the king from attacking the Shakyas. But the Buddha was unable to convince the king to transform all his hatred and desire for revenge, and eventually the king did kill almost all members of the Shakya family. On his return home, Vidhudhabha and his troops drowned in a river.

If we understand the law of karma, we realize that each individual, each family, each nation will reap the consequences of their deeds,

whether thoughts, speech, or actions. Although the Shakya clan produced a wonderful person who eventually became the Buddha and
preached that people should overcome caste and class barriers, they held
views in opposition to his teaching. They also deceived the king of Kosala, who was mightier than they. As for Vidhudhabha, his bad thoughts
led him to bad action and his life ended tragically.

How does this story relate to armed conflict in the modern world? For
Buddhists, the law of karma reminds us that when faced with violence
we must not react against it violently.[5] To quote a famous verse from
the Dhammapada:

> Hatred does not eradicate hatred.
> Only by loving-kindness is hatred dissolved.
> This law is ancient and eternal.[6]

Similarly, Mahatma Gandhi said, "An eye for an eye just makes the
whole world blind."

Not only Buddhists but Christians, Jews, and Muslims—all religious persons—need to be mindful when confronted with violence.
Then they can find the skillful means to deal with the situation nonviolently.

It is very important to understand that nonviolence is an effective
and very powerful response to conflict. Peace is not merely the absence
of war. Peace is a proactive, comprehensive process of finding ground
through open communication and putting into practice a philosophy
of nonharming and the sharing of resources.[7] Creating a culture of
peace is an active process.

When large-scale conflicts erupt, there is no question that they
demand a response. The problem is that many people believe that a
nonviolent response means doing nothing, and responding with force
or violence means doing something. The Middle Way of Buddhism
defines very well how one should respond to violence. It is about avoid-
ing extremes—neither doing nothing, on the one hand, nor responding with similar violence, on the other.[8]

We should not think of violence as limited to acts of war or terrorism. It is also important to examine *structural* violence, violence inherent in the very structures of our cultures and societies. Every day forty thousand people starve to death in a world where there is an abundance of food. The global economic system enriches a few while every day more and more people are pushed into poverty. Twenty percent of the world's population has over eighty percent of the world's wealth. In order for a few to enjoy wealth, others must be deprived of a decent livelihood. This is really one of the world's greatest injustices, the greatest act of violence. The problem with structural violence is that it is difficult to see. Many people dismiss it, saying that's just the way things are, or it's somehow unavoidable that things be this way. Similarly, many people dismiss nonviolence because they personally do not see how it can be effective. It does not attract as much attention as violence. Many people do not see how it can be a solution.

The roots of many global conflicts lie in structural violence. The economic forces of globalization, forced upon much of the world by the countries of the North, transnational corporations, and institutions such as the World Bank, the International Monetary Fund (IMF), and the World Trade Organization (WTO), not only condemn many to poverty but provide a breeding ground for hatred and greed, which in turn gives rise to violence. The demonic religion of consumerism is based on promoting greed, and in the name of this greed all sorts of violence is committed. The mass media, which are controlled by the transnational corporations (TNCs), are part of the problem of structural violence. They distort people's worldviews and preach the religion of consumerism. They work hand in hand with TNCs to promote a lifestyle of consumerism and create a global monoculture. Television effectively brainwashes people and acts as a propaganda machine for TNCs. It deludes people into thinking that the more goods they accumulate the happier they will be, even though such a consumer lifestyle is unattainable by the majority of the world's people and is an ecological impossibility, and to try to attain this unattainable goal inevitably leads to the perpetuation of this structural violence.

Nonviolence can provide a very effective response in situations of global conflict. We can define three types of response to global conflict: peacemaking, peace building, and peacekeeping. *Peacemaking* means keeping people from attacking each other. It is the process of forging a settlement between belligerent sides. *Peace building* refers to the entire range of long-term approaches to developing peaceful communities and societies based on principles of coexistence, tolerance, justice, and equal opportunity. *Peacekeeping* diminishes the most acute conflagrations of violence, and seems to attract the most attention but is a bit like firefighting. It's necessary to put out the fire of violence by keeping the peace, but it is much better if we can prevent the fire from starting. This is where peace building comes in. In addressing structural violence, conflicts can be prevented. Peace building initiatives can take many forms such as education, grassroots democracy, alleviating poverty, and land reform. These are all fundamentally nonviolent actions.

Thich Nhat Hanh, the Vietnamese monk who coined the term engaged Buddhism, says, "To prevent war, to prevent the next crisis, we must start right now. When a war or crisis has begun, it is already too late. If we and our children practice ahimsa in our daily lives, if we learn to plant seeds of peace and reconciliation in our hearts and minds, we will begin to establish real peace and, in that way, we may be able to prevent the next war."9 This idea of peace building, of *preventing wars before they begin*, is very important. This work attracts no headlines and in fact many never even notice it, but it really is crucial. Once a war has started it is difficult to stop. It requires much more effort and resources, and much damage is already done. Instead, we really need to start thinking about how we can stop the war that will start ten years from now. To do that, we must begin to create a culture of peace.

To create a culture of peace, first we begin by making society more just and give equal rights to all people. The imposition of "peace" is often a tool of suppression. Look at the many programs for pacification taken throughout the world. In many cases, the institutionalized definition of peace is tantamount to the suppression of struggles for equal rights and justice. In other cases, the institutionalization of peace is just propaganda for maintaining the status quo of an unjust government or system. Thus the development of a culture of peace really begins at ground level.[10]

The issue of economic globalization has been put firmly on the agenda by activists worldwide. Major protests against the WTO in Seattle, Prague, and Washington have forced a debate on the consequences of globalization. Media and governments can no longer ignore or dismiss these concerns. Working at the grassroots level is the key to ensuring lasting peace.

Peacemaking is the process of forging an agreement between two sides that are in conflict. The key ingredient is dialogue, and the most important part of a dialogue is listening. Unfortunately, much of the so-called dialogue that goes on in the world today is nothing more than two parties delivering monologues. Only through active listening can genuine dialogue occur. To engage in this active listening, we really need to have sown seeds of peace within ourselves. If we have seeds of peace then we can engage in this dialogue, this listening, without animosity or identifying things as good or evil, or parties as right or wrong. So for dialogue to be meaningful, both sides must be prepared to engage without preconceptions. They must give up any preconceived ideas about the outcome. If dialogue can be approached in this way, the outcome can be unexpected and wonderful for both sides.

Reconciliation is a key part of peacemaking. A peacemaker who can create a culture of truth, forgiveness, and cooperation can foster the acts of reconciliation necessary to bring about peace from discord. A culture of reconciliation is our best hope to heal past injustices and foster individual and societal transformation. Reconciliation simply means that both sides must have a willingness to forgive. While reconciliation acknowledges the past, it also acknowledges the need to live peacefully in the future.[11]

Peacemaking is an endless task. The work never stops—but that does not mean we should cease. One colorful image describes a peacemaker who, knowing that the well needs water, climbs up the mountain to the snow line, takes a spoonful of snow, and climbs back down the mountain to drop it in the well—only to climb back up the mountain for another spoonful. Because the need for peace is overwhelming we should never abandon our responsibility as peacemakers.[12]

Peacekeeping is more problematic. Although it is often done with good intentions, military-led "peacekeeping" simply uses the violent means of ordinary conflict for the goal of peace. While this form of peacekeeping may help minimize the magnitude of a conflict, it simply *cannot* lead to long-term peace.[13] Although peacekeeping may prevent violence in the short term, the important thing is to address the underlying causes of the violence. This is the only way to ensure lasting peace. It is important to recognize that some forms of supposedly nonviolent intervention are actually very violent. For example, trade sanctions against Iraq (a supposed means of keeping the peace) after the first Gulf War killed more people than the bombs had.

A true nonviolent response is based on *metta karuna*, or loving-kindness and compassion. The Dalai Lama uses the term "universal responsibility" to describe a sense of concern for the welfare of others.[14] "Universal responsibility" describes the motivation for a nonviolent response to conflict. The Quakers, for example, managed to break the food blockade against Germany and Austria after World War I, motivated by a sense of universal responsibility to the people of Germany and Austria. Thirty years later they were able to assist Jews inside Germany at the height of the war. They did not use threats of punishment or military might. They used only their love and concern for others as a motivation for their action. Because they intervened without threats, their presence was tolerated at a time of extraordinary violence.[15]

Small numbers of people have entered extremely violent situations with a nonviolent spirit, and have successfully tempered conflict with almost no personal casualties. These efforts, ignored by the mass media, are often carried out by idealistic individuals with very few resources.[16] Because they have accomplished so much with so little, just imagine what could be achieved if more people took this work seriously and if these individuals received the kind of support that conventional conflict resolution does. Usually such initiatives are tolerated by governments and other institutions; however, to follow this example further, the Quakers were condemned by the United States government for their evenhanded delivery of aid to North and South Vietnam in the 1960s.[17] This can be considered a form of structural violence perpetrated by the government of the United States.

Examples of the successful use of nonviolence are many: the nonviolent overthrow of the Thai dictatorship in October 1973, an event that resembled the demise of the Marcos government in the Philippines; the collapse of communism in Eastern Europe; Xanana Gusmao's command to Falintil to remain hidden in the jungle while Indonesian militias rampaged through the country after the referendum in 1999, and so many more. Nonviolence takes great courage. The image of a lone protester standing in front of a tank in Tiananmen Square and Aung San Suu Kyi confronting the Burmese military with great determination are two powerful reminders of the courage required to engage in nonviolence.

Although creating a culture of peace is most important, and prevention is better than any treatment, we still need to respond to violent situations in creative and nonviolent ways. Society invests so much in war and violence. If similar investments were made in peace and nonviolence, the results would be beyond imagination. As Mahatma Gandhi said, "We are constantly being astonished these days at the amazing discoveries in the field of violence. But I maintain that far more undreamt of and seemingly impossible discoveries will be made in the field of non-violence."

It is up to us to make these discoveries.

2. A Buddhist Perspective on Nonviolence

NONVIOLENCE IS NOT ONLY THE ABSENCE of violence; its meaning is much deeper than that. If one stands by and allows an act of violence to occur without intervening in some way, from the Buddhist perspective this can be considered an act of violence.

Samdhong Rinpoche, the Buddhist monk, scholar, and Gandhian who is *Kalon Tripa* (Prime Minister) of the Tibetan Government-in-Exile, has said that although the teaching of nonviolence can be explained in the phrase "Violence is not good," and the precept would simply be "Do…or practice no violence," it is not that simple. The scope and purpose of nonviolence and the way to put nonviolence into action is vast, and each individual can have a different approach.[18]

Thich Nhat Hanh is another eminent Buddhist teacher and proponent of nonviolence. His practice of Buddhism developed during the Vietnam War, a time of great suffering and violence throughout Vietnam. During the war, Thich Nhat Hanh realized that he could not remain in the monastery and meditate while bombs were exploding outside and people were dying. He could not turn away from the suffering of the world; he had to respond to it. Thich Nhat Hanh's nonviolent opposition to the war in his country was met with skepticism by both sides. The Vietnamese suspected him of collaborating with the Americans, while the Americans thought he was a communist. Thich Nhat Hanh's nonviolent opposition to the war in his country can in no way be considered a weak response. In fact, it was a response that demanded great bravery and courage.

All sects of Buddhism share five precepts of moral conduct. These are not strict laws but, rather, guidelines for an ethical life based on compassion. The first precept is not killing. This precept has at its roots both nonviolence and compassion. Here is Thich Nhat Hanh's version of the first precept: "Aware of the suffering caused by the destruction of life, I am committed to cultivating compassion and learning ways to protect the lives of people, animals, plants, and minerals. I am determined not to kill, not to let others kill, and not to condone any act of killing in the world, in my thinking and my way of life."[19]

For Thich Nhat Hanh, the true practice of not killing goes much deeper than merely refraining from killing at a personal level. If we are not mindfully aware, we can kill in many ways without knowing it, and yet this killing still has its roots in our minds. Hence, mindfulness is essential for the practice of nonviolence. Thich Nhat Hanh further explains, "We may be killing every day by the way we eat, drink, and use the land, air, and water. We think that we don't kill, but we do. Mindfulness of action helps us to be aware so we can stop the killing and begin saving and helping."[20] Implicit in this statement is the idea of structural violence, which I have mentioned in the previous chapter and will discuss more later.

In fact, all acts of violence have their roots in the mind. Obviously if we want to kill someone we need to carry out some physical action, but the intention to carry out this action must first arise in our mind. If we can be aware of the feelings that arise in our mind that lead to violence, we can better understand the root causes of violence, and better alter our intentions before enacting violence.

Thich Nhat Hanh founded the Order of Interbeing. This order has fourteen precepts. It is interesting that it is not until the twelfth precept that killing at the physical level is considered. The first precept reads, "Aware of the suffering created by fanaticism and intolerance, we are determined not to be idolatrous or bound to any doctrine, theory or ideology, even Buddhist ones. Buddhist teachings are guiding means to help us learn to look deeply and to develop our understanding and compassion. They are not doctrines to kill or die for." He explains further, "We usually think that killing occurs in the domain of the body, but a fanatical mind can cause the killing of not just one, but millions of human beings."[21]

So we see that in the Buddhist understanding, nonviolence—nonharming, or ahimsa—can be realized only through training our minds. Violence arises first in people's minds, and then in the world, because of anger, greed, and ignorance. Nonviolence arises through compassion— compassion not just for those close to us but for all life.

The question must be asked, How can nonviolence be applied in society? How can nonviolence be a solution to conflicts at a global level? Here we need to consider structural violence again. These days perhaps few of us kill beings directly, but we are all involved in killing through the products we buy and the lives we lead. Part of our taxes are used to fund the military, which is concerned, not at all insignificantly, with killing. So no matter how mindful we might be, or how well we might practice not killing at a personal level, we live in a world that is very violent. The nature of structural violence is such that many or even most people are not even aware of it.

In many ways our view of history is lopsided. It is a history of war and conflict. Many cities around the world have monuments to remember the many who have died in wars, but how many monuments are there to the heroes of nonviolent struggles? In many cases their names are not even recorded. Who was the lone protester standing before the tank in Tiananmen Square in 1989? Although the twentieth century was a century of conflict and violence, we should not forget the many nonviolent struggles that bought about greater peace and justice. The people-power revolution that overthrew the Marcos government in the Philippines, the civil rights movements led by Martin Luther King in the United States, the nonviolent resistance to the German occupation of Denmark in the 1940s, and the Solidarity movement led by Lech Walesa in Poland in the 1980s are just a few examples. These stories need to be told, remembered, and learned from.

My own country, Siam (which I refuse to call Thailand), has had three major nonviolent revolutions in recent history. The most recent was in May 1992. Unfortunately all these revolutions, despite their non-violent nature, were met with violent repression by the military, and many people were killed. It was only last year that an official monument was built to remember those who died twenty years earlier, on October 14, 1973. Many families still do not know the truth about what happened to their sons and daughters on that day.

It is also important to closely analyze the role of the mass media. Often the mass media merely beat the drum of war. They present war as inevitable or the only reasonable response. The response to the events of September 11 and the subsequent conflicts in Afghanistan and Iraq are cases in point. Little attention was paid by the media to attempts at a negotiated solution, yet the eventual bombing campaign against Afghanistan received blanket coverage. The mass media generally have too much interest in the status quo to meaningfully report on alternatives. This is not to denigrate the work of individual journalists, many of whom risk their lives, and even in some cases lose their lives, in an effort to find and report on the truth.

I would now like to examine more closely some examples of the power of nonviolence. These examples help to provide clear templates of how nonviolence can be an effective and powerful way of bringing about change in society.

Few conflicts are more prominent in the world than that between Israel and Palestine. For many people it would be unimaginable to set foot in this area of conflict, where bombs explode and bullets fly in every direction. But for activists from Gush Shalom, an organization promoting peace and human rights in Israel, the act of challenging the Israeli occupation of Palestine nonviolently is their life. Gush Shalom—represented by Uri and Rachel Avnery—was one of the recipients of the Right Livelihood Foundation's Right Livelihood Award in 2001 for its work in peacemaking in the midst of this bloody conflict. Uri Avnery received an unprecedented standing ovation for his speech on receipt of the award.

The methods of nonviolence used by Gush Shalom activists are many and varied. Gene Sharp wrote in his famous book *Politics of*

Nonviolent Action of the "198 methods of nonviolence." Perhaps the work of Gush Shalom could add a few more. Their work includes:

- rebuilding the houses of Palestinians destroyed by the Israeli army;
- filling in trenches dug by the Israeli army to cut off Palestinian villages;
- harvesting olives on behalf of villagers prevented by the settlers and the army from entering their olive groves;
- boycotting of the products of Jewish settlements on Palestinian land; and
- symbolic marking with green paint of all the points where the roads cross the Green Line between Israel and occupied territories, to signify to travelers that they are leaving their own country and entering the country of their neighbors.

Gus Shalom activists are regularly arrested and abused, although as Israelis their treatment is far better than that suffered by Palestinians. Their presence in conflict situations does much to prevent the mistreatment of Palestinians.[22]

Despite the terrible conflict that exists in Israel/Palestine, Uri Avnery is confident and optimistic that peace can become a reality there in the near future. His words demonstrate the progress that has been made toward an independent Palestinian state and its peaceful coexistence with Israel. "When we set out more than fifty years ago, there was hardly an Israeli who was ready to admit that a Palestinian people even exists, let alone that it had any rights. Only thirty years ago Golda Meir, then prime minister of Israel, declared that there is no such thing as a Palestinian people. Today, there is hardly an Israeli who denies the existence of the Palestinian people."[23]

There is of course no greater proponent of nonviolence than the late Mahatma Gandhi. Many of his nonviolent actions against British rule in India are well known. Gandhi also conceived the idea for Shanti

Sena, the Peace Army. He began work on this after he returned from South Africa to India in the 1920s and continued working on it throughout his life. In a bold but misunderstood proposal, he advocated that India respond to the anticipated Japanese invasion with nonviolent peace brigades during World War II. He even continued to advocate for Shanti Sena after independence—for example, in the dispute over Kashmir.[24]

Gandhi had little chance to test out these ideas himself because he was imprisoned by the British and received little support from his associates. However, the greatest peace army the world has ever seen was in the 1930s, in what was then known as the Northwest Frontier Province of India, organized by Khan Abdul Gaffar Khan. More than a hundred thousand men—all devout Muslims—vowed to resist British rule without weapons in their hands or violence in their hearts, and they kept their vow despite great provocation.[25] While Gandhi is known throughout the world and widely regarded as one of the greatest persons of the twentieth century, Khan Abdul Gaffar Khan remains virtually unknown. We must ask why this is.

In more recent history, groups such as Peace Brigades International have intervened in conflicts in Guatemala, Sri Lanka, Aceh, and elsewhere. The idea of civilian-based defense is attracting attention from some governments such as Sweden and Austria, but such a force is intended mainly as a method for resisting invasion. Sadly, the idea of peace armies or third-party nonviolent intervention has attracted little attention from governments or the media. Many proposals fail simply because of a lack of support, not because they are unworthy.

Four forms of third-party nonviolent intervention have been identified: accompaniment, interposition, observation/monitoring, and modeling.[26] *Accompaniment* has been successfully used by Peace Brigades International (PBI) in Guatemala, El Salvador, and Sri Lanka. International volunteers accompany local activists who are at risk of assassination. The volunteers focus international attention on the activists, and no activists have been killed while accompanied by the PBI. *Interposition* refers to a third force that physically intervenes to prevent two forces that are preparing to engage in violent conflict. *Observation/monitoring* is often used in elections where violence is expected. Observers do not usually intervene in the conflict, but their presence reminds people that the world is watching and helps to restrain violence. *Modeling* involves individuals or teams entering a conflict situation and, through body language and words, assisting people to choose nonviolent behaviors or behaviors that reduce violence. Likewise, practices such as active listening help promote a sense of mutual respect and transform attitudes toward conflict.[27]

These methods all demonstrate the ways in which nonviolence can reduce conflict. Undoubtedly there are others. Yet they all suggest that ordinary people can nonviolently intervene in conflicts, successfully reduce the level of violence, and begin constructing peace.

Should we say that nonviolent intervention is an idea whose time has come? In fact it is an idea whose time is long overdue. How many more people have to die in violent conflicts before we adopt real alternatives? We cannot leave this vitally important work up to governments. There are just too many vested interests that would never allow this work to be done effectively. Yet nonviolence is work that can be achieved by ordinary people. For example, a nonviolent peace force of two hundred peace workers and five hundred support staff could operate on a budget of eight million dollars a year. While this sounds like a lot of money, it is equivalent to what the world spends on the military *every four minutes.*[28]

The examples of nonviolence I have given represent only a small fraction of what nonviolent action can achieve. While the scale of global conflicts is often overwhelming, an extraordinary amount can be achieved with comparatively few resources. There is a saying, "There is no way to peace, peace is the way."

3. The Real Crisis in the World

ISLAM TEACHES PEACE and nonviolence. It is lamentable that many mainstream scholars accuse Islam of being one of the root causes of violence in the world, including the September 11 terrorist attack on the United States. The attack seems to confirm the "clash of civilizations" thesis of Samuel Huntington. Building on Huntington's thesis, some have even argued that World War III—a war between the West and non-Western civilizations—will break out within the next twenty-five years. The September 11 terrorist attack is the first catalyst of this next world war, or so the argument goes.

It is unfortunate that the American ruling elites are paying even a modicum of attention to Huntington, who is a false and dangerous prophet. It must be remembered that in the 1960s Huntington advocated massive American bombing of Vietnamese rural areas in order to drive villagers into government-controlled areas. There the refugees would be awestruck by the material benefits of urban life. They would then develop modern values and turn their backs on communism, Huntington contended. It takes quite a talent to overlook the consequences of this policy. South Vietnam was strewn with dead bodies. The Thai military dictatorship participated in this "noble" cause, providing bases for American warplanes to pound Indochina to pieces. Before returning to the Thai bases, American warplanes generally emptied their bomb loads over Laos. It is estimated that the total tonnage of bombs dropped over Laos is greater than that dropped over Japan during World War II.

The United States might have superior technological and military power, but it could not legitimize the American invasion of Vietnam.

A similar case can be made about the American attack on Afghanistan, and, of course, Iraq. Both countries have been battered by all kinds of bombs, including the breathtakingly "dumb" cluster bombs, and its entire population is being held hostage for defying America. The majority of the victims of the Anglo-American attack are innocent people— just like the victims of the World Trade Center attack. It should be pointed out that no Afghans and certainly no Iraqis participated in the September 11 attack. Most of the terrorists were Saudis.

The United States was quick to occupy the moral high ground, insisting that its attack on Afghanistan was a just war, a moral crusade. Bin Laden's "admission" that he ordered the terrorist attacks against the United States lent further credence to the American position, or so the apologists for the Anglo-American violence believed. But this "hard" evidence became available only *after* the United States unleashed the dogs of war in the Middle East. Before the Anglo-American attack, the lack of even a shred of hard evidence was deemed immaterial.

How many times has the United States committed atrocities in the name of pious principles? The postwar record of American foreign relations sheds much light on why numerous peoples worldwide hate the United States. Recall the Suhartos and the Pinochets of the world. These brutal tyrants were all supported by Washington during the cold war. It did not matter that they came to power by military *coups d'état* or other illegal means. It did not matter that they perpetrated atrocities and nefarious acts of aggression against neighboring states (e.g., Suharto's invasion of East Timor in 1975), thus violating international law and the UN Charter. As long as they were subordinate client states, Washington was willing to turn a blind eye to their actions. Conversely, independent nationalists who legitimately came to power by free elections were often targets of American subversion.

It is well-known that Bin Laden was once on the CIA payroll. His service was needed to fight the Afghan leaders sponsored by the USSR. Saddam Hussein, now portrayed as a virtual reincarnation of Hitler, was once a client of Washington—until he committed the crime of insubordination by invading Kuwait. The Anglo-American sanctions (under the fig leaf of the UN) against Iraq deprived the Iraqi people of basic necessities and led to the death of over half a million Iraqi children due to starvation and easily preventable diseases. Though each American casualty in the war in Iraq is amply recorded in the American media, little is heard even of the number of Iraqi casualties, as if to say that the Iraqis are unworthy victims.

What about the Taliban who came to power in Afghanistan in 1996? Did Washington see the Taliban as a rogue regime from the outset? Did Washington complain about how the atrocious Taliban did not allow Afghan men to shave their beards? As the British journalist John Pilger observes, "When the Taliban took Kabul in 1996, Washington said nothing. Why? Because Taliban leaders were soon on their way to Houston, Texas, to be entertained by executives of the oil company Unocal. With secret U.S. government approval, the company offered them a generous cut of the profits of the oil and gas pumped through a pipeline that the Americans wanted to build from Soviet central Asia through Afghanistan."[29]

Small wonder that now, to replace the Taliban, a "moderate" set of leaders is needed to protect American oil interests in Afghanistan.

The response to the September 11 attack is illustrative of how violent responses are the inevitable product of violent systems. George W. Bush argued that the terrorists attacked the United States because they envied the freedom and prosperity in the United States. This is a fallacious and conceited view. At present, blinded by vengeance, patriotism, and imperial hubris, the American mainstream mass media are engaging in self-censorship or news distortion, parroting the official line. Moreover, had the terrorists really envied American liberty, we might well imagine they would have attacked a more relevant symbol of that ideal, say, the Statue of Liberty. That they chose to destroy the World Trade Center and the Pentagon suggests that they opposed capitalism and the American military-industrial complex, two leading causes of violence throughout the world.

The September 11 terrorism raised many questions for thought. If only the American ruling elites—and those throughout the world—

could reflect critically on this act, wisdom and compassion might emerge instead of vengeance and hatred.

The United States decided to go its own way (i.e., more violence) in avenging the attack, bypassing the UN and making a mockery of international norms. The Bush administration clearly stated that it would act unilaterally if no other states chose to side with it. This is the logic of a violent superpower, the logic of violence itself.

If the United States and its allies want to assume global responsibility, they must first cultivate mindfulness and use ahimsa as guidance. They must derive their leadership from legitimacy, compassion, and justice, not from military might. The more the United States uses its power illegitimately, the more its standing as the self-designated leader of the world will be repudiated and undermined.

The state of the world in the years following September 11, 2001 indeed constitutes a crisis. It should be noted that the word "crisis" comes from the Greek *krisis,* which means "to separate," with the implication of "choice." And it is very true that America and the world face a choice. If American leaders come to understand terrorism as a cost and consequence of American imperial practices (admittedly a very big if), and if they shun violence and pursue a policy grounded in non-harming rather than structural violence, the United States can redeem itself. If not, it is likely to face more of the same tragedy in the future. Peace means not only the absence of war but also the presence of *metta, karuna,* and wisdom.

4. Culture and Reconciliation

CULTURE IS SUCH AN INTANGIBLE NETWORK of beliefs, rituals, language, and history that I hesitate to begin with a definition. Similarly, reconciliation is a concept that constantly evolves and adapts to changing situations. What is clear is that a culture of truth, forgiveness, and cooperation can foster acts of reconciliation, which in turn can bring out the life-affirming aspects of culture. A culture of reconciliation is our best hope for healing past injustices and fostering individual and societal transformation. To explore the themes of anger and reconciliation, let us look at several examples from recent history.

In recent years, South Africa has been in the world spotlight. After apartheid ended, legal and political changes were implemented, but devising a strategy for social change is more difficult. The Truth and Reconciliation Commission was formed in South Africa under Archbishop Desmond Tutu in order to make public the crimes that were committed under apartheid. The commission set out to hear the cases of aggressors—both those in government and in the opposition—as well as their victims. Those who came forward with confessions have largely been granted amnesty, and many victims have been given compensation. The reparations are meant to restore a sense of dignity to victims of human rights violations and to demonstrate a commitment to a more just social order. The commission has made the transcripts of the hearings and the decisions to grant or deny amnesty available on the Internet, and is working in conjunction with Amnesty International to prevent future violations of human rights. The Truth and Reconciliation Commission was a groundbreaking initiative to promote forgiveness and justice after much past hatred. Now, years later, can we say that the commission has helped the reconciliation process?

The evidence is difficult to decipher. It is clear that, in its attempts to reveal the truth about human rights violations, deep wounds were reopened and the process seemed to nourish anger and frustration rather than reconciliation. With the worsening poverty in Soweto and other black townships, the granting of reparations seemed to lose its symbolic value. Crime has worsened and, along with it, disillusionment and hopelessness among black and colored citizens. Many whites have become more fearful and have fled the country. I will address the question of what can we learn from this situation at the conclusion of this essay.

A lesser-known case of attempted reconciliation centers on the Pak Moon dam in Siam. The construction of this dam, situated in Ubon Ratchathani Province at the confluence of the Moon and Mekong Rivers near the border with Laos, destroyed five villages and the livelihoods of thousands of fishermen and their families. Despite years of protests, the dam was completed in 1994 and the residents were displaced with the promise of reparations, which have not been delivered. After the dam was operational, thousands of villagers continued their struggle by erecting a number of protest villages near the dam and setting up a camp in front of the Government House in Bangkok. In Bangkok, the villagers tried to voice their concerns and make officials and citizens aware of their cause. They organized themselves as the Assembly of the Poor, a people's organization committed to representing the voices of the poor. During the decade of protests, the Assembly of the Poor succeeded in using academics and NGO (nongovernmental organization) staff as resources rather than looking up to them as leaders, in accord with the principle of bottom-up emancipation.

The dam has disappointed even its most enthusiastic corporate sponsors. A recent commission jointly established by the World Bank and NGOs has declared the dam a disaster on many levels. The *Bangkok Post* reported:

Today, what is left of the once abundant and peaceful riverside villages is the grand edifice of the Pak Moon dam, which has been described by the World Commission on Dams as a financial and environmental disaster.

According to the commission's study, the 136-megawatt dam can produce only 21 megawatts of electricity. Out of 265 fish species recorded in the Moon River, only 96 remained after the dam was completed in 1994. The rapids were destroyed forever. The artificially created "fish ladder"—meant to allow fish to swim upstream of the dam to spawn—does not work. Income from reservoir fishing is exaggerated while the catch upstream of the dam has declined by 60–80%.

The remarkable fact is that the community of displaced people mobilized itself in two parallel ways: as a political protest movement and as a creative venture in self-reliance and sustainability. Both streams were committed to incorporating spiritual practice and a goal of contentment rather than material wealth. As part of the movement for self-sustainability and community well-being, participants launched several initiatives that have improved the quality of life for many of the villagers:

- A group was formed to open a traditional health-care center that offers herbal saunas, traditional massage, and medicinal herbs to the members of the settlement.
- Several community businesses have emerged. These businesses produce for their own consumption and sell only the surplus, thus meeting the needs of the members and reducing the amount of money flowing out from the community. Income-generating enterprises include the production of natural shampoos and dishwashing liquids, herbal teas and medicines, natural vegetables, microbe fertilizers, soymilk, and vegetarian food; an

experimental enterprise has been set up to market these
products among the urban middle class, especially
hand-woven and naturally dyed cotton products, and
to encourage small-scale farmers to convert from
industrial fertilization to organically grown rice.
- A youth environmental group was established.
- A preschool center run by volunteer teachers was built.

These initiatives were geared not only toward self-reliance and sustainability but also democracy—a point that is often missed by mainstream observers or commentators. However, the efforts of the villagers
were thwarted again. In November 2000 a fire of unknown cause
destroyed part of the settlement community. The Electricity Generat-
ing Authority of Thailand (EGAT), the owner of the dam, admitted
it had hired people to "politely request the villagers to vacate the location." These hirelings used gasoline to destroy two hundred homes and
the local school.

At one point, a large number of unnatural fish deaths were discovered in the water near the dam. It appears that some type of toxin or
poison had been put into the water with the hope of killing the fish.
The villagers brought evidence of this destructive act to the provincial
government asking for an explanation. Even today, the villagers await
a response.

Despite all the obstacles to the people's movement, there has been
progress. The media played an important role in supporting the hope
that the government can change its policy about the poorly performing dam. I remember during a television forum addressing this issue a
deeply moving outcry of hope and determination from the crowd of
villagers the moment that I proposed that the dam be destroyed. Since
then, a new Lower House has been elected and a new government
formed under Prime Minister Thaksin, which claimed they would take
the villagers' concerns seriously.

In April 2001, the government and members of the Assembly of the
Poor held a series of important conversations about the needs of the

displaced villagers. They agreed that all eight gates of the dam would be opened for four months while an ecological impact study was being conducted. The cabinet also agreed to the following:

- A commission will be set up to consider complaints on other dams.
- Villagers who lived in the forest that has since become a protected area will be allowed to return.
- Small fishermen will be allowed in marine national parks.
- The minister of justice will ensure that the more than 100 lawsuits against the Assembly of the Poor will be handled fairly.
- All field trials of genetically modified crops will be suspended, and a biosafety act will be drafted with the participation of farmers, consumers, and academics.

Wanida Tantiwittayapitak, adviser to the Assembly of the Poor, said that the time was right for an agreement to take place. She said, "It is about time to go home. If the villagers stayed here a little longer, they would become urbanites. Indeed, they have started scavenging for recyclable garbage. That is a sign of becoming urban poor." Her comment may provide insight into the case of South Africa, where urban poverty overwhelmingly affects the black community. As Wanida said, urban poverty has a dehumanizing effect. Scarcity, despair, and alienation from nature create a culture of "kill or be killed," and individualism seems the only strategy for survival. These situations have a deep need for a culture of reconciliation, and it must come through skillful means. Truth, forgiveness, and renewed strength must be fostered, provided they are grounded in indigenous traditions and wisdom.

By taking control of their lives and their community, feelings of bitterness and anger in the Pak Moon community are balanced by a spirit of hope and empowerment. Through various administrations, the anonymous nature of government made it difficult for fruitful discussion to occur between the government and the residents of Pak Moon. After the government agreed to their demands most villagers tried to be hopeful, but they remained skeptical. One woman admitted she had little faith that the demands of the Assembly of the Poor would be realized, but also said, "I have hope for this government. They have talked more to the poor in their first two months in office than the previous government did in four years. If this government cannot make change, then I doubt that any government will."

The plight of poor agricultural communities was a large issue in the 2000 national election, and the Thai Rahk Thai government won based on its populist platform. The villagers saw that this government had a vested interest in assisting them, but unfortunately the Thaksin administration has not followed through with its claims to respond to these villagers needs. The villagers and members of the Assembly of the Poor have become frustrated with the government's mishandling of these problems. This frustration is turning to desperation and anger.

Anger is a feature of human experience and should not be ignored or suppressed. It is an important component in the process of reconciliation. For reconciliation to occur, it is necessary to express and understand anger without judgment. The move from anger to reconciliation requires mindfulness. Mindfulness is a process of awareness and consciousness that helps us to see the reality of interconnectedness and the universality of suffering. When we have this realization, we see that anger directed at other living beings is futile and we are called to act with compassion. The path of mindfulness and realization is not necessarily a linear one. Along this path are periods of stagnation, failed attempts, and retrogression to anger and despair—we must be prepared for this. When we have setbacks we depend on our friends, allies, and supporters to help us through it, and our awareness of interconnectedness is strengthened.

The villagers at Pak Moon and the Assembly of the Poor are conscious of this fragmented process. They are honest about the futility of talks with previous governments, but still see the need to fully commit to engaging with the government. They see obstacles as part of the ongoing process. It is more difficult to understand how the violent acts of EGAT are part of reconciliation. Yet, even when confronted with the challenge of the burning of homes and the poisoning of water, non-violence in thought and speech emerges as the wisest response and the right way to keep on the path.

Since misinformation and propaganda is a big source of frustration and anger for the villagers, full disclosure is an important component of reconciliation. One man said, "The government is not sincere and hides information. They only publicize good things. Villagers are dissatisfied with misinformation and the violations that come from misinformation." The need for a clarification of misinformation is very similar to the logic of the Truth and Reconciliation Commission in South Africa. The report of the World Commission on Dams has provided the scientific evidence for the villagers' version of the truth. In discussions with the current government, the report helped persuade bureaucrats and politicians that the plight of Pak Moon is creditable.

Reconciliation is the awareness of interconnectedness that leads to creative innovation. The construction of the dam illuminated the dependent co-arising of all sentient beings at Pak Moon. The cooperation of the government and EGAT is needed to restore this interconnectedness and revive the villagers' culture and dignity. Innovation and creativity are crucial elements in reconciliation. Forgiveness and a correction of past wrongs are not enough; there must be cooperative efforts at constructing a new and better reality.

The issue of collective guilt has received much attention since World War II and has been applied to German and American military aggression. Collective guilt may be a necessary stage in reconciliation: People should face the truth and take responsibility for their wrongdoing, but guilt can become a paralyzing force that prohibits growth and reconciliation. If a particular ethnic group or race is identified as guilty, individual power seems irrelevant and personal acts of forgiveness seem to have no place. A mentality of collective oppression and victimization is a dualistic way of thinking, and dualisms or binary distinctions—good/evil, East/West, knowledge/intuition—are obstacles to insight and action. From a nondualistic perspective, we are all both aggressors and victims. We must be mindful about how we can best affirm life and foster compassion in the family, community, and world. Reconciliation thus entails understanding the many causes of hatred and greed in the world, acknowledging the shared struggle of humanity in overcoming them, and translating this awareness into life-nurturing actions, which include everything from daily acts of kindness to improvements in health, education, and housing. What is implicit in any act of reconciliation is the idea of being part of a greater whole, a web of interconnected relationships. Each being in this web of relationships is like a jewel in the net of Indra, each jewel reflecting the beauty and radiance of every other.

Reconciliation requires seeing the world as it is, not as we wish it to be. We cannot make compassion dependent on an ideal of some wished-for world. If we hope to influence the real events of our world, we must be realistic. We need to see that even the most flawed people have Buddha-nature, and reconciliation begins with the acknowledgment of common humanity and shared suffering. This means we cannot let our ego get in the way and get caught up in the idea that we are superior to others and have a responsibility to teach them or forgive them. Social transformation begins with our ability to understand our relationship to others and transcend our pride and delusion.

The case of racial reconciliation in South Africa and the loss of livelihood at Pak Moon are very different examples of the need for reconciliation. The reconciliation that is occurring in South Africa is more complicated than Pak Moon, and I do not mean to imply in this essay that the strategies used in Pak Moon would automatically be appropriate for South Africa. Rather I bring up both of these examples to illustrate our need to move beyond the dualistic idea that reconciliation merely implies forgiveness or compensation between oppressors and victims. The case of South Africa is a testament to the fact that political changes and monetary compensation alone cannot transform deep-seated anger. There must be a spiritual component as well, and this must occur in the individual, family, community, and

nation. Our common project must be to nurture this spiritual transformation in ourselves and our communities so that we can address
the urgent needs for political and social reconciliation, and create the
foundation of a more just society.

5. The Value of Simplicity and Humility

I AM SOMETIMES ASKED—or ask myself—what I, as an Eastern Buddhist, expect Westerners to discover in the Buddha. This is a difficult question. First, there is the customary problem of division and hence of imagining the West and representing the East. In other words, there is the pitfall of *"I* think, therefore *they* are"—in this case, a kind of Occidentalism that serves only to stereotype Westerners and Eastern Buddhists alike. Aside from having to deal with the inaccuracy or slipperiness of any form of representation, the implication or logical culmination of this view may be racism, including the paternalistic kind. Once you say "I am," "you are" and "we" and "they" naturally follow; conflict and fragmentation then ensues, which is not healthy for the cultivation of the whole unit, both individually and collectively. The second problem, which derives from the first, is that the question treats Westerners as a homogenous or unitary entity. And lastly, in this era of transnationalism, the fate of many "Easterners" and of many "Westerners" may be similar. For instance, a powerful transnational capitalist class seems to be emerging whose members are composed of elites and professionals in the North and the South, the East and the West.[30] They engage in similar patterns of accumulating capital, consuming, and thinking. Thus any geographical, cultural, or racial categorization may be artificial and pointless.

Rather than dwelling on the simplistic East-West dichotomy (or any other one!), I focus on some pervasive and disturbing transnational developments. I humbly and sincerely insist that these negative trends can be overcome by discovering the teachings of the Buddha.

In the post–Cold War world, a spirit of "capitalist triumphalism" is overwhelming many capitals and leaders worldwide, breeding hubris, delusion, and arrogance. It is particularly strong in the West, which has allegedly won in the battle against the Communist monster. The aggressive, if not coercive, promotion of "free market" capitalism in the form of neoliberalism is a stark manifestation of capitalist triumphalism. As John Ralston Saul has pointed out, a new Holy Trinity has been erected, consisting of competition the Father, efficiency the Son, and marketplace the Holy Spirit.[31]

In the current capitalist ethos, tolerance for socioeconomic diversity and alternative models of development is low to the point of being nonexistent. The global economy is the only future. Refusing to accept this rationale is taken as a sign of weakness, immaturity, and inferiority. It is argued that we are at the highest mark of human development and civilization, and this often unspoken sentiment prevents the peoples of the world from pursuing other aspirations and from thinking about alternative ways to improve or maintain their livelihood. The global economy does not really cherish a diversity of ideas, cultures, aspirations, and views—only a diversity of products. The diverse ways of life worldwide increasingly dance to the same tune of consumer culture, which insists that ultimate happiness can be achieved by the never-ending consumption of goods and services. Needless to say, this oppressive environment is like a tightening noose that will squeeze the life out of meaningful freedom, democracy, and human rights.

I encourage people worldwide, especially the ones who are propagating or indoctrinated by capitalist triumphalism and consumerism, to look to the life example of the Buddha—and to see him simultaneously as one who reached the pinnacle of liberation through his enlightenment, and also as a simple and humble monk. In fact, simplicity and humility *enabled* the Buddha to achieve enlightenment.

By simplicity, I mean the freedom from attachment to physical and sensual pleasure. We have to understand that all gain, honor, sensual happiness, and praise ultimately lead to loss and suffering. The Buddha called these states of mind the eight worldly conditions and stated that whoever is enslaved by any of these shackles will never be free from the cycles of birth and death. Simplicity contributes to the realization of a noble life and to living nobly because it guides us down the Noble Eightfold Path.[32] Contrary to the rationale of consumerism, where *more* is considered *better* and where the amount of personal gain and possessions marks the goodness of one's life, one learns from the Buddha to constantly reduce one's attachments and to envision the good life as the successful overcoming of attachment to gain. Free from these attachments, one has the time and energy to nurture the seeds of peace within, and thereby in the world.

With a proper understanding of simplicity, one leads a peaceful life and relates harmoniously to all sentient beings and the natural environment: one does not abuse them in one's thoughts, speech, and actions by indulging the senses. For example, if one upholds simplicity, one will understand that consumerism endangers the biosphere and strengthens the transnational corporations that give primacy to the accumulation of profits over people's well-being. One is mindful of how to create wealth and how to make use of it. One learns to give more than to take. One's simple yet harmonious lifestyle merges with goodness, engendering a pure form of beauty that paves the way to enlightenment.

The twin of simplicity is humility. By humility, I do not mean merely the opposite of vanity or arrogance—because all opposites contain each other. One cannot know humility only by rejecting pride, because tension, conflict, and confusion are inherent in all forms of *becoming* and *being*. The very process of *becoming someone* must be negated in order to really reside in peace. I assert that this peace can be attained through a process of mindful breathing and meditation. However, the negation of becoming and being runs counter to the basic Western philosophic notions of freedom and progress. Small wonder that many experts in socioeconomic development once condemned Buddhism as antithetical to modernity!

To relate this conception to the current economic trend, Buddhists would argue that "small is beautiful."[33] This maxim meshes with other values such as self-reliance and self-sufficiency. Furthermore, environmental sustainability and socioeconomic justice are more conceivable when growth is tempered or limited, when humility and simplicity are promoted. The insatiable quest for profits and greater returns to shareholders, on the other hand, propels corporations to globalize their businesses and investments at the expense of the environment and communities whenever they can get away with it. Moreover, transnational corporations propagate the ideology and culture of consumerism, which is the basis for their existence and prosperity. Of course, transnational corporations often profess a concern for the natural environment. But you never hear them say that the root of the environmental crisis is endless consumption. They say instead that the natural environment will be sustainable once we all learn to consume *differently*. If we consume "environmentally friendly" products, for example, everything will be all right; every environmental problem will be manageable. But an increasing number of researchers are pointing out that consumerism and unlimited growth directly contradict the very idea of environmental sustainability. Some of these people even promote the idea of a post-development society and suggest abandoning the concept of development.[34] At best, technological advancement can only delay the impending ecological disaster. As one scholar of globalization rightly questioned, "Is global consumerist capitalism, as represented by the practices as well as the policies of corporations, sustainable?"[35] Put differently, we have to ascertain whether or not the whole international capitalist system itself—its agents, institutions, structures, and culture-ideology—is inherently defective. From a Buddhist perspective, it definitely is.

Like simplicity, humility implies the respect for all beings. Once we are humble, we coexist with one another as equals. The belief that one is exceptional or superior, for whatever reason, is a major wall that hinders meaningful and compassionate human and social relations. Blinded by exceptionalism, one sees the world in absolute terms. If one is always right or good, then the others are always wrong or evil. Hence, to right the wrongs one can take whatever measures one wants. Only when this dichotomous wall is torn down will we really begin to *see* the consequences of our actions. Moreover, if we value equality we will not treat the suffering of marginal individuals or groups with callous equanimity. Rather we will struggle for greater social justice. Equality does not always have to mean sameness; it can also refer to justice. Equality mediated by justice requires treating people differently under different circumstances, such as providing unequal shares to unequals.

Moreover, equality tends to denote a "leveling-up" process, like, for instance, emulating the rich and powerful. Here, however, we seem to forget that if the rich were to turn toward simplicity and share their wealth with the poor, thereby becoming more like them and "leveling-*down*," equality could also be attained. Mahatma Gandhi has famously said, "There is enough in the world for everyone's need, but not for some people's greed."

With humility we will be able to transcend racial, national, cultural, ideological, and religious boundaries (real or imagined) and form a circle of the virtuous, or what the Buddhists called *kalyanamittas*. Now this is tremendously important because some of the most threatening menaces to human well-being and environmental sustainability are transnational in character. The circle of the virtuous must be extended to incorporate members of the power elites, of the transnational capitalist class. If we treat them as friends, not as enemies or demons, we can embark together on changes that, however incremental, will awaken the humanity—as opposed to the half-humanity of the economic man, the nationalist, and all the other ignorant impulses—in us all. We need not be dialecticians to understand that transnational cooperation, in particular the bottom-up kind, is facilitated by the very same forces that lubricate the wheels of globalization.

The etymological meaning of the word *buddha* is "to be awake." Once we are awakened to the virtues of simplicity and humility, to the suffering engendered by greed, hatred, and delusion, our consciousness is "restructured." We become "mindful" of others and ourselves, and we begin to restructure human society. The restructuring of human consciousness and that of society are necessary and complementary.

Consider this story from the sutras: One day a leader of a religious sect came to visit the Buddha and asked him, "If I follow your way, what will I do day by day?" The Buddha replied, "Walk, stand, lie down, sit, eat, drink." The religious leader then inquired, "What is so special about your way?" And the Buddha answered, "It is indeed special. The ordinary man, though he walks, stands, lies down, sits, eats, and drinks, does not know he is walking, standing, lying down, sitting, eating, and drinking. But when we walk, we know that we are walking. When we stand, we know that we are standing." The point of the story is to show the virtue of mindfulness. Once the human consciousness is restructured, the world is perceived nonjudgmentally, that is, without division and conflict.

Both simplicity and humility, which the Buddha exemplified, remind us that Buddhism is not really concerned with the private salvation of the individual. Moreover, the concern with individual salvation is a form of self-interest, which ultimately puts limits on compassion and love. Individual salvation may be a high form of self-interest, one that it is not so worldly and so on, but it is self-interested nevertheless. And like all forms of self-interest or attachment, it narrows the range of thoughts and feelings. For instance, the preoccupation with private salvation leads to attachment to one's beliefs, faith, teacher, hope, etc. and may foster the intolerance of other faiths, beliefs, and teachers. This way of thinking breeds division and conflict not dissimilar to nationalism, racism, and other -isms. Thus the preoccupation with private salvation dulls and tethers the mind, making real freedom impossible. Freedom entails the unfettering of the consciousness from its attachments, values, and judgments—indeed from all its contents.

The crux of the Buddha's teachings transcends the notion of individual salvation and is concerned with the whole realm of sentient beings or the whole consciousness. Here the inescapable conclusion is that Buddhism requires an engagement in social, economic, and political affairs. One cannot overcome the limits of the individual self in a selfish and hermetically sealed manner. Lamentably, the global economy props up the ego especially by making a virtue of greed and consumerism.

The wheels of the global economy are fueled by insatiable greed. The Buddha, on the other hand, taught that the wheel of righteousness *(dhammacakka* or *buddhacakka)* must control or influence the wheel of power *(anacakka)*. In the contemporary world, the quest for greater profit ultimately determines the actions of the rich and powerful, taking precedence over other motives. Therefore, any top-down attempt to redress class and ecological problems is likely to fail; at best it will only be a palliative. The teachings of the Buddha, however, state that the rich and powerful, especially the rulers, must have only one overriding concern, that of upholding the law of *dhamma.*[36] The virtues and duties of any ruler are spelled out in detail in the Pali canon as follows: generosity, high moral character, self-sacrifice, honesty and integrity, gentleness, self-control, patience and tolerance, forbearance, and conformity to the law. The same logic applies to the ethical code for the Buddhist lay community. The more one strives for enlightenment and the well-being of all sentient beings, the better. But it is all too human to fail.

In conclusion, I want all those (not just Westerners) who are captivated by the culture and ideology of consumerism and indoctrinated by the belief in the linearity of history to see the Buddha as a simple and humble monk. The teachings of the Buddha, if properly understood and upheld, provide a different lens to see the world. These teachings have been applied for centuries and are interwoven into the Vinaya, the rules of monastic conduct, which still guide the spiritual growth of modern Buddhist communities.

I feel that the upholding of the Vinaya may have a great demonstration effect and trigger profound and long-lasting social change. As the late Thai monk and social activist Buddhadasa observed:

I won't be able to overturn the land [i.e., sweep up all the mess and begin with a clean slate]. I can only do it gradually as permitted by my intelligence and energy. However small the end result of my contribution, I am satisfied. But I am hoping that many people will think positively of my action, which reflects my dedication to Buddhism, and will emulate it. Soon individuals in powerful positions or people all round the world will do it, and there may be something akin to the overturning of the land. Even though I did not overturn the land myself, the end result would be the same. I still remain modest and humble and will not be overwhelmed by the feat ahead of me."

6. A Simple Monk

THE DALAI LAMA often introduces himself as "a simple monk," even though he is a head of state as well as a special spiritual leader within the Vajrayana Buddhist tradition, and is believed by many to be an emanation of Chenrezig, the bodhisattva of compassion. I find it meaningful and touching that the Dalai Lama—a title meaning "Ocean of Wisdom"—describes himself with such unpretentiousness. This reflects his humility, but it is also significantly truthful.

A few years ago, a Christian group circulated leaflets outside a large public meeting in Honolulu. The leaflets suggested that since the Dalai Lama refers to himself as only "a simple monk," then why should people respect him? What can he do? Instead, the people should turn to Jesus, who was not only the *Son of God* but also the *Savior of the World.*

On the other hand, both in public as well as in private, the Dalai Lama has often praised Jesus, Mohammed, and many other religious leaders. He encourages the Christians and the Jews to practice their own religions wisely and mindfully. If they want to add Buddhist meditation to their spiritual traditions, it is all right, provided they do not belittle their own religions.

Another simple monk, my own late teacher, Bhikkhu Buddhadasa, asked all his followers to live by three important guidelines: Try to understand the essential teachings of the Buddha and put them into practice as selflessly as possible; respect and honor our friends' religions, not regarding them as inferior to our own; and unite with those of other faiths and nonbelievers so together we can overcome greed, hatred, and delusion.

Bhikkhu Buddhadasa dedicated himself to work as the servant of the Buddha, and this is in fact what the name "Buddhadasa" means. The Buddha himself was a simple monk. We may recall that when the Buddha was a prince, he reveled in all worldly pleasures, shielding himself from suffering in the world. Eventually, he managed to witness an old man, a sick man, a dead man, and a monk. Suddenly, it dawned on him that sickness, death, and suffering are inextricable, and he wanted to overcome them. He felt that abandoning sensual pleasures and becoming a simple mendicant might be a way to overcome suffering. The Buddha-to-be was a wandering monk for six years before he could awaken from greed, hatred, and delusion. His understanding was so thorough that no selfishness was left behind. As a result, his wisdom was transformed into compassion.

For many Buddhists, being a simple monk (or a simple nun) is essential for a person to achieve the highest goal in life—overcoming suffering and being in the state of real happiness without depending on sensual or external conditions.

If we do not lead a simple life, we get preoccupied with so many things that we have little energy left to concentrate on mindfulness, and understanding of the reality of all mental and physical phenomena and the "mysteries" of the universe. While scientific knowledge helps us understand some aspects of the universe, only deep meditation free from selfishness will help us realize the truth.

Unfortunately, some monks who have left the mundane world to pursue the truth are still caught up in gratifying their thirst for sensual pleasure. Some lose their willingness to live simple lives, and become obsessed with fame and wealth. They are monks in name only; they no longer lead a noble life.

Morality, or ethics, is said to be the foundation of the successful development of the human potential. According to the Buddha's teachings, living within the discipline of the vows of morality—commitments such as not harming any living being with one's body or speech by not lying, not killing, and not stealing—is the most effective way to accumulate the positive karmic energy of morality: a buildup of positive habits of mind, body, and speech.

Such vows or commitments are not moralistic restrictions but practical guidelines for life. Laypeople have their own unique sets of vows, but the vows of monks and nuns are said to serve as the most potent way to live within the commitments of morality. Fully ordained monks, for example, have 227 vows. The more vows one has and keeps, the easier it is to develop our innate potential for love, kindness, patience, and wisdom. And it is common sense that one is more likely to succeed in something by devoting more time to it and by living in an environment that supports the endeavor.

A simple monk endeavors to attain and uphold upekkha, which is tragically lacking in our violent world. Upekkha, the fourth of the brahmaviharas, is defined as equanimity, neutrality, or poise. Venerable P. A. Payutto, a leading Thai monk, explains upekkha as "seeing things as they are with a mind that is even, steady, firm, and fair like a pair of scales; understanding that all beings experience good and evil in accordance with the causes they have created; [and the readiness] to judge, position oneself, and act in accordance with principle, reason, and equity."

Venerable Payutto describes upekkha as the attitude of someone who—although greatly concerned that individuals within his charge are safely and effectively performing their own duties—knows how to simply look on with detachment, without bossing them around or interfering. Such a person is like a carriage driver who, when the horses are running smoothly and on course, sits quietly and alertly. A more comprehensive definition of upekkha, paraphrased from the *Visuddhi-magga*, is to passively watch when others are able to take responsibility for themselves, or when they deserve the results of the actions for which they are responsible.

A point that needs to be stressed is that upekkha does not mean sitting on a fence and doing nothing—hermetic isolation, apathy, insensitivity, let alone criminal negligence. Upekkha calls for mindful (temporary) detachment to cultivate wisdom; the latter is a precondition for helping others with compassion and understanding

In sum, a simple monk is someone who is ever humble, mindful, and leads a noble and celibate life. He wants so little for himself that all his time and energy are sacrificed for the happiness and welfare of other sentient beings. His happiness depends on his thoughts, his speech, and his actions, which are directed first and foremost to the well-being of others. His life is harmonious physically, mentally, and spiritually. And this harmony leads to harmonious relationships with other monks and nuns, as well as to laypersons. His lifestyle influences the laity, who try to imitate the simple mindful living of the monks. His lifestyle also influences natural phenomena, making them more harmonious and wholesome. Even beasts and bees learn to be less harmful and more compassionate! The simple life of a monk can contribute much to social welfare and environmental balance. Moreover, a simple monk has time for learning various sciences, which can prevent as well as cure modern personal or social ills. We can look to the example of His Holiness the Dalai Lama to see this at work. During the last few years, the Dalai Lama has engaged in fruitful dialogue with leading scientists and doctors to explore the intersection between Buddhist wisdom and medical science. These dialogues have led to many interesting discoveries concerning the nature of the mind and the value of meditation practice in health care.

Some political tragedies such as the Chinese invasion of Tibet are damaging and horrendous. It is illuminating to hear simple monks like the Dalai Lama and his followers insist that we all can learn to love and empathize with the Chinese people and forgive the Chinese government for its acts of aggression, committed out of delusion, greed, and hatred.

Even when a simple monk is tortured physically or mentally he practices his mindfulness of loving-kindness and compassion. Although the Dalai Lama has not been tortured physically, he suffers mentally every time he learns the hard fact that lay followers, monks, and nuns in Tibet are being tortured mercilessly. Yet he bears this pain magnanimously.

And he reminds us all that the only way to overcome suffering is to cultivate seeds of peace within and to work nonviolently and patiently. The Dalai Lama has shown to the world that truth, beauty, and goodness are not only possible but also practical. Although he travels around the world to meet people of all walks of life, he still manages to hold spiritual retreats, perform ceremonies, and teach young monks to walk the Noble Eightfold Path of the Buddha.

I believe that the Dalai Lama's influence in the world is not due to his being regarded as an incarnation of a bodhisattva, or as a head of state in exile, or a spiritual leader of a large Buddhist community. Nor is it because he possesses any supernatural powers that make him fundamentally different in nature than the rest of us. Rather it is because he is a simple monk who wants so little for himself and is devoting so much of his time and energy to help the peoples of the world, who are being trammeled by greed, hatred, and delusion.

He desires only happiness and well-being for all, and he shows them that the highest happiness depends on simplicity, truthfulness, and compassion. With seeds of peace within, a simple monk like His Holiness is in an excellent position to guide others who are aspiring for world peace, social justice, and environmental sustainability. Let us strive to learn from his example.

Simplicity,
Compassion,
and Education

7. The Virtuous Friends of Christianity and Buddhism

UNDERSTANDING THE UNIVERSAL VALUES inherent in all religions includes appreciating the unique strength of each. Accepting these differences and the process of change and transformation can lead to better cooperation and a renewed commitment to social justice. Robert Traer, a theologian by training, cautions, however, that selectively extracting thoughts from religious teachings in order to show their similarities can be disrespectful to people who have a total commitment to a particular faith. Teachings must be understood within the larger context of faith, and more important than the teachings are the believers and their daily application of the teachings. For communities of believers, religion is not just a resource for achieving a balanced spiritual life; it is the essential ordering of all life. Traer suggests that we would gain more from talking about faith in a personal and experiential way rather than in terms of theory. This experiential approach to interreligious dialogue, with its connections to flawed institutions, historical conflict, prejudice, and so forth, is a place of meaningful exchange.

In the model of the life of Jesus, Christianity offers all religions an enormous gift. From a Buddhist perspective, we can see how the life and teachings of Jesus also exemplify the two highest values in Buddhism, wisdom and compassion. The compassion of Jesus toward the sick and the poor and his ability to refrain from judgment parallel important qualities of the Buddha. Historically, Christian missionaries in Tibet recognized that the teachings of Christ were similar to those of the Buddha. In their view, Buddhism promoted an inferior worldview of ignorance and superstition. It might be said that when Gautama became enlightened and realized ultimate reality, that he gained certain "god-like" qualities. But we should not synthesize unique aspects of different religions, equating some aspect of one with some aspect of the other. If we allow ourselves to be comfortable with differences, we will have a richer understanding of divine reality. In this way, we can move forward as equal partners in the shared struggle to overcome ignorance and suffering.

Although the scriptures about Jesus and the Buddha offer models of a spiritual way of life, cultural and historical factors influence how they are interpreted. Buddhist scriptures have been approached critically from many perspectives including those focusing on race and gender. Scriptures and teachings are deeply connected to social structures, and violence committed in the name of faith cannot be ignored.

The Christian scriptures have also been critiqued and reinterpreted, not only in academic or theological exercises but also through daily practice and worship. The process of critical analysis does not detract from the value and truth of religion; indeed, I assert it is necessary for its survival. Reinterpretation and criticism is a process that must go on within us. Acknowledging our own prejudices and insecurities is part of our growth; it adds to our humanity and ability to connect with others.

When I was at the UN Summit for Spiritual and Religious Leaders, I was saddened by the apparent arrogance of many of the representatives. Each person seemed to seize upon time at the microphone and the opportunity to give an uninterrupted monologue detailing all the tenets of their personal faith system. Although this is sometimes inevitable in large conferences, it is nonetheless a loss to everyone. Those of us in this field are particularly vulnerable to delusions of grandeur and, often, to loneliness. In a Buddhist worldview *kalyanamittas*, or virtuous companions, are crucial to spiritual growth. Friends are the only people who can give us the criticism and the support that we need to transcend our own limitations and can comfort us if we fail. If we become so self-absorbed that we do not have kalyanamittas in our lives, we stagnate in complacency and self-righteousness.

The Theravada Buddhist community in Siam is going through a period of reinterpretation and growth accompanied by turmoil and uncertainty. One contested area is the movement to reestablish the tradition of *bhikkhunis* (nuns) in Siam. Although there are Buddhist nuns in Japan, Taiwan, Korea, and Tibet, Siam has only a weak female monastic presence. The status of women who wish to ordain is low, and very few nuns have the opportunity for higher study in the dhamma or secular subjects. Often, nuns are reduced to serving the needs of monks and must do the cooking and cleaning at the monastery. A nuns' college has been formed, and although this is a valuable step to empowering women and nuns, many people in leadership are not ready for a change in the structure of ordination and in the relationships between *bhikkhus* (monks) and bhikkhunis. The government does not provide ordained women with the benefits of free transportation and health care as allowed for monks nor does it give them the political right to vote as laity.

In 1996, the Theravada bhikkhuni lineage was reestablished in Sri Lanka after a nine-hundred-year absence, and Sri Lankan bhikkhunis are already respected in society. They are well educated in secular and religious disciplines and involved in community projects. As ethnic conflicts continue in Sri Lanka, female monastics are an important force for peace building. However, monastic isolation cannot lead to inner contentment, and ordained people must work to lessen the material and spiritual suffering of others. In January 2001, the Ariyavinaya conference was held in Siam. Fifty representatives from around the world, including monks, nuns, academics, economists, and artists, gathered to discuss ways to transform their Buddhist faith into a more engaged form that confronts poverty, violence, and consumerism.

The need for reform within the *sangha* (the monastic community) was emphasized, and there was a consensus that guidelines were needed for monastics in their use of technology and forms of entertainment, management of finances, and involvement with the lay community. On one hand, puritanical views about monastic life can lead to backlash and corruption, but on the other hand, a set of rules is mandatory; the monastic community should set a moral example for the rest of society and show that a life based on material consumption is not the only option. An example of this conflict can be seen in the film *The Cup*, which is about teenage monks who devise a plan to watch the World Cup final on television, and can be seen from both perspectives. The young monks are more interested in television than anything in the monastery, including its rules. They appear to be totally under the influence of technology and entertainment. But in the final scene it is clear that the values of friendship and cooperation among the monks is more important than a soccer match played in a far-off land.

Engaged Buddhists can also learn from other faiths. The Quakers, officially known as the Religious Society of Friends, have been a constant source of inspiration and support in my life and my work as an engaged Buddhist. I have learned a great deal from them, especially from their honesty, simplicity, and commitment to nonviolence. They not only practice nonviolence but also confront reality and oppose war in a nonviolent way. These peace churches continue to play an important role in speaking the truth about power. They are an important model for engaged Buddhists, who often preach nonviolence, but have not confronted structural violence in a very meaningful way.

One of the biggest challenges all religious communities must tackle is hierarchical systems. For many Buddhist believers, hierarchical structure means that relations between ordained people and laypeople are based on sacrifice and superstition, rather than cooperation. Community festivals are one way to foster cooperation and celebration. I recall participating in a forest robes ceremony at Wat Padad, a forest monastery located three hours from Chiang Mai. The religious ceremony, part of a two-day festival held at the monastery, included food stalls, handicraft demonstrations, games organized by the local school, and a children's dance performance. For a brief time, the monastery was again a central space for the whole village, and there was an evident sense of pride in local traditions and a respect for nature as a symbol of the history of the community. This sense of community interconnectedness and respect for nature is difficult to cultivate in a world where individual wants are supreme. Constant desire and a loss of control over individual and communal circumstance are marked effects of life in the twenty-first century. Amidst this feeling of chaos comes a great need for spirituality.

Communities of like-minded people must unite. It is time to bring discussions of spirituality into the domain of economic development and education. The Spirit in Education movement (SEM) in Bangkok has recently opened a new office in Chiang Rai, in the north of Siam, and will work to connect with organizations and individuals interested in progressive environmental education. The SEM is also trying to build an alternative education resource center.

I have been inspired by many Christians whose devotion to their faith is intertwined with their commitment to social justice. The theologies of liberation articulated by Gustavo Guttierrez in Peru and many others in South and Central America are inspiring in their passionate commitment to the needs of the poor and oppressed. Dialogues among leaders in the Christian community and liberation theologians about Marxism, economic justice, and social responsibility have helped to bring Christianity back to one of its original aims of alleviating the suffering of the poor.

The Christian socialist tradition of Reinhold Niebuhr and his critique of both capitalism and Marxism are still applicable today. In his book *The Children of the Light* Niebuhr wrote that one Marxist illusion is "that the inclination of men to take advantage of each other is a corruption which was introduced into history by the institution of property. It therefore assumes that the socialization of property will eliminate egotism." He goes on to say, "A second source of Marxist illusion is its belief that the ownership of property is the sole and only source of economic power." From a Buddhist perspective, private property is not the primary source of egotism. Pride, craving, and attachment are internal qualities that exist with and without private property. External factors are manifestations of internal chaos, but material change does not necessarily lead to inner transformation. Buddhism says we must tackle these inner obstacles nonviolently and patiently.

Similarly, cultivating compassion in all relationships is necessary to catalyze change in oppressive power structures. Focusing only on equality in distribution does not entail a change in the relationship between producer and consumer. Buddhism advocates a change in the way we view and appreciate material goods and understand the co-arising of mind and matter.

Economic power is not the only source of power. We all have the power to cause suffering in relationships and cannot attribute this only to the social structure. The need for power stems from a desire to feel superior in the vain quest to establish a unique self. Buddhism teaches that there is no such thing as the isolated self; our entire reality is made up of nonself elements. Thich Nhat Hanh calls this concept "interbeing." From the perspective of interbeing we are all both the oppressor and the oppressed, the producer and the consumer, the Buddhist and the Christian, and our worldview cannot be dichotomized to include only one aspect of our reality. Economic relations have come to dominate other relations, which forces people to define themselves by how much they own—money, possessions, and people. But when we define ourselves as part of a web of relationships, the quality of our interactions and our ability to temper hatred, greed, and delusion emerge as the highest values of existence.

Interreligious exchanges are beneficial reminders that although freedom and happiness seem like intangible goals compared to the very concrete goals of corporate globalization, many people of diverse traditions are committed to this same objective. With kalyanamittas, the transformation becomes easier and our purpose—to extend the spirit of compassion and justice to others—becomes clear.

8. A Very Simple Magic

A MONK WENT TO SEE THE BUDDHA and told the Awakened One that he had meditated for many years to develop the magical power of walking across a river. The Buddha commented on how silly that monk was to waste so much time to achieve something so pointless. The Buddha recommended that if the monk wished to cross the river, the best way to do so was to get a boatman and pay him a few coins.

In Buddhism, magic does not mean walking on water or flying through the air. It is rather considered magical—miraculous—to walk on earth mindfully. If we do not exploit the earth, nature will care for itself, and contribute to the human effort of growing physically, mentally, and spiritually.

When we look at a flower mindfully, we will realize a very simple magic: the flower has non-flower elements. Right now it is fresh and beautiful, but soon it will decay and die. It will become compost and will be reborn as a plant, which will again produce flowers for all those who appreciate beauty and goodness. This is magical indeed. Likewise, each of us will one day die, and our dead bodies will unite with the earth, and rebirth will take place. Without *you*, there could not be a *me*. You and I inter-are, as Thich Nhat Hanh puts it. In each of us, there are non-human elements. We are the sun, moon, earth, river, ocean, trees, etc. Without all these other objects, we human beings cannot survive.

Scientific knowledge conditions humans to be like machines, and to perceive the world and the universe as merely composed of matter. From this perspective, matter has no life or feeling. Hence we destroy

Mother Earth and cut down trees for financial gain or in the name of economic development.

Although the destruction of nature by humans has been a problem for ages, the problem was compounded during the Age of Enlightenment, when the philosopher Descartes argued, "I think therefore I am." With this statement, it was assumed that any being that cannot think is inferior and can therefore be exploited by those who can think. Even among thinking beings, the more clever ones who can think better are in a position to exploit the weaker ones.

Besides, the more we concentrate on thinking, the more our thought becomes compartmentalized. The deeper we think, the more we bury our thoughts and ourselves. We cannot see the forest for the trees. We are unable to perceive the world holistically. Hence we do not question the products of our thinking and our experiments with matter.

An even greater problem has come with the age of consumerism which goes by the name of globalization. We have now changed the phrase "I think therefore I am" into "I *buy* therefore I am." Lulled to sleep, most people in this age of consumerism have only two aspirations in life, to earn money and to consume whatever advertisers tell us to buy. Advertisers are on the whole controlled by transnational corporations, which have become more influential than any nation state, and whose main objective is to exploit natural resources and human beings in the relentless pursuit of economic gain.

If one were to go to the Buddha to ask for a solution to the problems resulting from Cartesian dualism or corporate consumerism, one that might help us rid ourselves of all the modern predicaments, I imagine he might suggest "I breathe, therefore I am."

Breathing is the most important element in our lives—indeed for any living being. It goes on day and night, twenty-four hours a day, seven days a week. Yet most of us do not take good care of our breathing. If we did, that would indeed be a simple magic. I quote from Thich Nhat Hahn:

Breathing in, I calm my body.
Breathing out I smile.
Dwelling in the present moment,
   I know this is a wonderful moment!
Breathing in, I know that I am breathing in.
Breathing out, I know that
   as the in-breath grows deep,
   the out-breath grows slow.
Breathing in makes me calm.
Breathing out makes me feel at ease.
With the in-breath, I smile.
With the out-breath, I release.
Breathing in, there is only the present moment.
Breathing out, it is a wonderful moment.

The above technique is called *samatha bhavana*, or the development of calm abiding, which helps one to be tranquil and to plant the seeds of peace within. After developing this, one would develop *vipassana bhavana*, insight meditation, in order to develop a critical awareness of the self and take it less seriously. Thus one becomes less and less selfish, and one looks for peace and justice in the world—with real understanding of oneself and of the world. Hence one is no longer controlled by biased views of love, hatred, fear, or delusion. Our magical formula could go like this:

Let us pray for world peace, social justice, and
   environmental balance, which begin with our own
   breathing.
I breathe in calmly and breathe out mindfully.
Once I have seeds of peace and happiness within me, I try to
   reduce my selfish desire and reconstitute my consciousness.
With less attachment to myself, I try to understand the
   structural violence in the world.
Linking my heart with my head, I perceive the world

holistically, a sphere full of living beings who are all
related to me.

I try to expand my understanding with love to help build a
more nonviolent world.

I vow to live simply and offer myself to the oppressed.

By the grace of the Compassionate Ones and with the help
of good friends, may I be a partner in lessening the
suffering of the world so that it may be a proper habitat
for all sentient beings to live in harmony during this
millennium.

Indeed, the heart of Buddhist teaching has much to do with social
ills. The Four Noble Truths—suffering, the causes of suffering, the
cessation of suffering, and the path leading to that cessation of suffering—can be skillfully applied to social activism. This too is indeed
a very simple magic. Moreover, through deep breathing one can see
how social suffering arises from the three roots of evil, namely, *lobha*
(greed), *dosa* (hatred), and *moha* (ignorance).

In our personal lives, understanding the three root causes can help
us to rid ourselves of pain and disturbance. In the social context, they
help us to envisage causes of structural violence and offer us hints
about how to respond.

Consumerism and capitalism are the most prominent modern forms
of greed. We try to fill the gaps in our hearts through ever-increasing consumption and accumulation. Failing to understand the magic of adver-
tising, we are at its mercy. This inevitably leads to conflicts of interests,
and inevitable exploitation. Militarism embodies hatred as its core basis.
The lust for power, which leads to widespread human-rights abuses, is a
prime example of how hatred can manipulate individual minds and lure
them to install unjust social structures.

The third root cause, ignorance, is perpetuated by centralized education. Students are taught not to think holistically, but to compart-
mentalize their thinking, to memorize, and to abide by the existing
norms. This helps to explain the weak mobilization of the student
movement and other social movements. Oftentimes, students are trained

and equipped only with the skills they need to become employees of multinational companies, where, once hired, they exploit their own fellow nationals and the country's natural resources.

All this suffering can be reduced or totally extinguished by the right understanding of the nature of things. The Buddhist approach is unique, for it is reinforced not by faith but by practice. To attain understanding, one must actually experiment with the truths themselves. Aloofness is never a value that Buddhists praise. Buddhism can give one a sense of "interbelonging," in which one feels the interrelatedness of all beings, and recognizes how one belongs within it. It helps to remember that we all are "friends in common suffering," as a common Buddhist phrase goes.

Thus, my Buddhist model of development must begin with everyone practicing to understand himself or herself. In the Buddhist tradition, we call it *citta sikkha*, or the contemplation of the mind. Meditation is important for us to attain insight, which has the qualities of alertness and criticality. Critical self-awareness is important for Buddhists. Beginning with a critical understanding of oneself, we try to reach a critical understanding of our community, society, nation, and eventually our world. We develop a critical awareness of society and the government, and we examine all established institutions in order to understand how the mechanisms of greed, hatred, and ignorance operate at the structural level of society.

Buddhist tenets also help me feel closer to and identify with other sentient beings. In the Buddhist tradition, we believe that every being embodies a Buddha nature, or the potential to attain the highest understanding. Thinking this way, I feel the equality among all of us regardless of rank and status. And I feel that the poor are entitled to the same dignity as the rich and powerful when they struggle for what they should have been given.

My projects during the last thirty years have sprung from this thinking. We started working with local people in Siam and then expanded to the international level. For example, I felt interested in working with the Thai Buddhists in my country some thirty years ago, and later on founded the Thai Inter-Religious Commission for Development (TICD) to implement training to raise the awareness of monks and nuns about social and environmental issues. In the last ten years, I co-founded the International Network of Engaged Buddhists (INEB) to spread the ideas of socially engaged Buddhism at the global level, and to tap support for the Buddhist minorities in Bangladesh, India, etc.

Buddhist teaching is the core that permeates all my activities. It is indeed a very simple magic, which starts with proper breathing. Incorporated in this magic is the voice and wisdom of people at the lowest level of society—monks in Asian countries often come mostly from the lowest background. I also feel that beauty has to go hand in hand with all activism. I have made all my efforts to preserve ancient artifacts and mural paintings, and I have also used culture and the arts as a tool to prompt social and political change. Culture in my view is not bounded by national borders; it reaches out to one's neighbors and beyond. So we should have respect for other cultures, traditions, and religions precisely because it is only through tolerance that society will find peace. A diverse and vital culture lies at the heart of the struggle against the monoculture that flourishes today. This work grows out of the very simple magic offered by the Buddha.

9. Compassion or Competition

MANY OF YOU HAVE MADE a commitment to move beyond a purely economic motive in conducting your businesses. You have an understanding of the interconnectedness of all people and the need for a sustainable relationship to the environment. This understanding is part of a new vision, one that cannot be quantified in terms of monetary profits and losses and that does not consider wealth and status as the key to happiness. This is a tremendous shift in thinking with far-reaching implications.

His Holiness the Dalai Lama teaches eloquently about this topic. *Compassion and Competition* is the title of a book based on a forum with His Holiness held in the Netherlands in October 1999. Compassion and competition are not mutually exclusive. His Holiness has said, "Any human activity carried out with a sense of responsibility, a sense of commitment, a sense of discipline, and a wider vision of consequence and connections, whether it be involved with religion, politics, business, law, medicine, science, or technology—is constructive." The emphasis is on the motivation for action. Because motivation is closely connected to an individual's worldview, any change in worldview, such as an understanding of interdependence or the universality of suffering, will lead to a change in motivation. As motivation shifts and the sense of responsibility and commitment is strengthened, broader changes can take place. For example, when a motivation for profit shifts to a sense of concern for the economic and spiritual well-being of the employees, a cooperative relationship can replace an exploitative one.

Similarly, competition is not a singularly negative force. In moderation and with a sense of direction it can be used to push us to become kinder and more generous. His Holiness makes the distinction between two kinds of competition when he says that one kind of competition seeks individual glory whereas the other kind includes an awareness that other people must be nurtured or empowered. Competition can be beneficial if it inspires us to be the best we can in order to serve others. Rituals and games, although often competitive, can serve to strengthen the spirit. This discussion of competition and achievement parallels the discussion among Buddhist scholars about the purpose of *nibbana* (nirvana, or enlightenment). For some, spiritual enlightenment is a personal quest. For others, such as those in the engaged Buddhist community, true enlightenment is built upon wisdom and compassion and is intrinsically connected with the well being of all. The Mahayana tradition is particularly emphatic that all beings must be liberated before the bodhisattva attains enlightenment. These discussions about the nature of competition and nibbana highlight how a seemingly minor difference in focus can bring about a shift from an ego-centered attitude to a community-centered philosophy.

The local currency movement is one manifestation of a new formula of competition and compassion. The Bia Khud Chum is the local currency of a small village in Northeastern Siam. It is used for local transactions and to provide interest-free microcredit to villagers. The proposers of the Bia Khud Chum state that the local currency is not meant to isolate the village. Instead, it is meant to strengthen the economic foundations of the village by making residents aware of local production and increase community trust and social capital. It is not meant to replace the baht; like most of the two hundred local-currency communities worldwide, the Bia is used largely for services. A system of local currency may not be appropriate for all small communities, but all can still use the organization and commitment behind it as a model for structural change.

In a panel discussion with His Holiness, a managing partner at PriceWaterhouseCoopers, a financial corporation, spoke of a triple bottom line: financial performance, environmental performance, and social performance. If this concept can take hold in more corporations, this will be a huge step forward. Basing decisions on the triple bottom line is an explicit pledge to take responsibility for the effects of economic decisions. The essence behind this concept of the triple bottom line has historically been a very important part of Tibetan philosophy. In the Tibetan tradition, anyone who proposes a new invention must guarantee that it is beneficial or at least harmless for seven generations before the innovation can be adopted.

I spoke of a new worldview that encompasses far more than economic performance. This new worldview requires a transformation of self-goals and a new lens for understanding the problems of structural violence, environmental degradation, and consumerism. This new lens requires us to look beyond a traditional cost-benefit analysis and accept that everything has multiple causes and innumerable effects. As His Holiness says, "One of the characteristics of the modern Western approach to issues and problems is the tremendous emphasis on clarity and precision. But the problem that arises with an emphasis on precision is that our outlook narrows, because precision can only be found if the focus is narrow. Looking at the same issue from a wider perspective means that one cannot demand the same level of clarity and precision." As I see it, a lesser emphasis on clarity and precision does not mean that we cannot approach possible solutions with a critical eye and high standards.

We must maintain our high standards, but we must also be accepting of different representations and ideas. For example, a new World Bank report entitled "Voices of the Poor" includes many quotes from poor people and shows a willingness on the part of the bank to at least listen to the poor. Corporations are also realizing the need to have outside assessments of programs and performance. The benefits of external evaluators are well known, and in corporations that are making the transition to a new "triple bottom line," the comments of an outside party are even more valuable. Drawing external observers and evaluators from different parts of society can also promote compassion and competition.

The practice of making charitable donations or forming partnerships with nonprofit organizations is not a new idea. It is not enough, however. Merely making charitable contributions does change the focus or motivation of a business. Only when companies listen deeply and respectfully to other organizations can there be true integration of competition and compassion. Once formed, relationships with external organizations should be consistent and oriented toward the long term.

Nurturing a thriving arts community is one possibility for cooperation between businesses and cultural organizations. An emphasis on material success and earning power has taken resources and attention away from artistic communities. Creating and appreciating art is one of the ways we nurture ourselves and cultivate balance. Many people involved in social change work at a frenzied pace, trying to keep up with scores of activities and events. When we fail to attend to our own needs of inner calm, rest, and creativity, we are useless as agents of change.

I have offered some criticisms of the current model of corporate growth and globalization. We must now decide how to transform our commitment to social and environmental responsibility into practical change. Self-empowerment, community change, and a commitment to the arts are all part of a holistic transformation. An integrated model of competition and compassion is within our reach. Let us work together to achieve it.

10. Blessings and Courage

THOSE WHO ARE TRULY HUMBLE value simplicity. Those who are considerate and courteous to every sentient being, and to everything within their environment, are likely to attain the four blessings as enumerated by Theravada Buddhism:

Longevity: This does not simply mean living to a ripe old age. It means knowing *how* to live. Many people who are, for example, insincere, dishonest, selfish, greedy, and exploitative may well lead long lives. But they are far from experiencing the blessing of a worthy, spiritually prosperous, and noble life, one that emphasizes generosity, morality, compassion, and peacefulness. Such people are unlikely to relish the beauty of good living and the power of life.

Complexion: Internal and external conditions are intertwined. Those who know how to lead a good life will, it is said, have a healthy and beautiful complexion, which naturally reflects the radiant state of mind and patterns of behavior. A clear complexion indicates that the individual is living harmoniously with others and with the natural environment.

Happiness: Simply put, happiness or fulfillment is attained by promoting the happiness of others. When someone clearly sees that the majority of people in the world are suffering from grinding poverty, famine, preventable diseases, oppression, war, and so on, that person will dedicate his or her life to eradicate or mitigate these root causes of suffering, to create a more just and humane society nonviolently.

Strength: Needless to say, the blessed individual has spiritual and physical strength—i.e., the moral courage and physical endurance to nonviolently challenge the oppressive socioeconomic structures and concentrations of power. The individual will collaborate with others to realize this end, despite the great costs or risks involved.

I have sought to redefine and clarify the meaning of the four blessings in contemporary context. No one can grant these blessings. They can be engendered and nurtured only from within. The cultivation of mindfulness and simplicity is the cradle of the four blessings.

The highest form of blessing in Buddhism is known as *appama-dhamma*. I shall clarify on this matter by dividing it into two points.

Yonisomanasikara, or wise consideration: Anyone who seeks to attain the special blessings must begin by practicing mindful breathing in order to develop critical reflection or wise consideration. The individual should be ever mindful, recognizing whenever lust, hate, anger, vengefulness, obsession, and so on arise. With mindfulness, the individual may be able to overcome these impurities of thought, if only partially. The simple goal is to foster and nourish inner peace—to cultivate seeds of peace within—and further culture the mind (*bhavana*) to develop selflessness. After all, one must live life for the well-being of other people and sentient beings, not to mention the natural environment. Selflessness combined with an understanding of unjust social structures will engender solidarity and fraternity. Individuals will come to care about, promote, and benefit from one another's well-being; they will also nourish diversity in human relations with the natural environment.

Kalyanamittata, or virtuous friendship: Kalyanamittata is an external source of dhamma and nurtures our moral conscience. Spiritual friends raise embarrassing issues that we may not want to hear and remind us of the benefits of selflessness and goodness.

Religious leaders can easily fall prey to hubris or arrogance. Not infrequently they cave in to the seductive lure of the state, money, or fame, and then turn a blind eye to the suffering of the poor and marginalized. Some of them have ostentatious and luxurious lifestyles. Put simply, they do not live what they preach. If we become good companions to such religious leaders, they may rediscover the virtue of humility and simplicity and refrain from hypocrisy. They may even feel empowered and refuse to cringe in the face of political and economic power.

World religious leaders endowed with such blessings will have the courage to admonish or criticize the United Nations. They will point out that as long as the UN continues to cower in subservience when the lone superpower and great powers act unilaterally or violently, the organization will become a hollow, meaningless forum where small states can blow off steam. For instance, when the major powers obstreperously pursue the arms trade, the UN must exhort them to curb their activities.

Another pressing issue is China. Amnesty International has declared that no single person in China is immune from state-sponsored human-rights abuses. Yet the United Nations has allowed China to play a major role in running it. Beijing, for example, successfully pressured the UN to obstruct the participation of His Holiness the Dalai Lama in the Millennium World Peace Summit of Religious and Spiritual Leaders in August 2000. That His Holiness is a devout and humble Buddhist leader who strongly advocates the quest for truth and justice compassionately and nonviolently is beyond any doubt. If the UN consistently allows member states with vested interests to get the better of it, it will lose its credibility, and its espousal of global peace, justice, and prosperity will be mere rhetoric. If the present UN secretary-general sees us as his kalyanamittas, seriously considers our warnings, and consequently works to redirect some of the organization's activities, then the prospects for realizing these noble causes may be a bit brighter.

We must likewise act as kalyanamittas for the delegates of UN member states, sincerely pointing out that almost every government in the world is a primary cause of its citizens' destitution and its environmental degradation. This is, in part, because most governments, willfully or not, surrender to the dictates of transnational corporations, the World Bank, and the IMF, institutions that are driven by insatiable greed, capitalism, technological determinism, and consumerism.

If these delegates observe the warning flags that we have raised, they may also hear the cries and demands of the poor, weak, and marginalized. They may even revise their prejudices and attitudes and come to an understanding of the virtue of simplicity and humbleness. As such, they may begin to realize that the poor have much of value to teach. By organizing from the bottom up—that is, empowering grassroots movements and communities—and forging networks of alliances with the middle class and some political elites, we will strengthen the culture of peace. The greatest blessings are always the ones we cultivate within ourselves.

11. Buddhism and Environmentalism

BUDDHISM HAS BEEN CONCERNED with caring for the natural environment for over twenty-five hundred years, and there is a wealth of academic and spiritual literature on the topic. Buddhists have a responsibility to share their knowledge in this time of global environmental degradation. Recent protests have put the issues of globalization, capitalism, and the exploitation of labor and resources into the limelight. Many people are now willing to think about new paradigms for development and sustainability, and to form meaningful alliances on the path toward greater harmony with nature.

The concept of interdependent co-arising is the crux of Buddhist understanding. Nothing is formed in isolation and, like the jeweled net of Indra, each individual reflects every other infinitely. Attachment to an atomized sense of self and a self/other dualism are the antithesis of interdependence and is an obstacle to achieving the peace of enlightenment. A commitment to nature and a deep respect for all life can help foster a change from an individualized self to a self as interbeing. The well-known Vietnamese monk Thich Nhat Hanh uses the term "interbeing" to describe a self made up entirely of nonself elements including conditions and relationships. To acknowledge these nonself elements is to realize how one's survival and ability to flourish are entirely contingent upon the quality of engagement with other sentient beings.

The Buddha's teachings can be divided into teachings about the nature of suffering and about the ending of suffering. The development of wisdom and compassion are part of the path to the ending of suffering; the three sources of suffering are greed, hatred, and delusion.

Delusion can take the form of attachment to self, ego, money, or power, and can also be the belief that humans are the highest form of life and should view all other forms from a solely functional perspective. An attachment to scientific advancement and information technology as the keys to progress and happiness is yet another form of delusion. Frustration and futility are by-products of delusion. Some people fear that once they understand the reality of the world and the universality of suffering, they will be overwhelmed by the amount of work to be done and the level of commitment required. This paralysis is itself part of a delusional view of success, results, and pride. A societal change toward a more holistic view of nature will likely not occur in our lifetime. Just as the journey toward nibbana takes precedence over the end result, we must have faith in the journey toward a more interdependent worldview. Success comes in the form of small victories, individual transformation, and the strength of relationships.

a new view of success

Interpretations of suffering and realization are often used in conjunction with other nature-specific references in Buddhist texts to create a philosophy of Buddhist environmentalism. The following excerpt is from the Metta Sutta, an important ritual prayer in the Theravada tradition:

> Whatever living beings there may be,
> Whether they are weak or strong, omitting none,
> The Great or the Mighty, medium, short, or small
> The seen and the unseen
> Those living near and far away
> Those born and to-be-born—
> May all beings be at ease!...
> Even as a mother protects with her life
> Her child, her only child
> So with a Boundless heart
> Should one cherish all living beings.[37]

True equanimity does not lead solely to tolerance or nonharming, it leads to something much greater and more demanding—it leads to the nurturing love of all living things.

Dharma Rain is the title of a collection of essays that includes sacred texts that emphasize a reverence for life, nature as teacher, and the nature of nature. Rain is a powerful metaphor for the Buddha's teaching about the equanimity of life in all its forms. In the delicate balance of nature, all sentient beings benefit from the life-giving power of rain, each taking only what is needed and sharing the surplus.

The change of the seasons is a testament to temporality and the inevitability of change, death, and rebirth. Death in the cycle of nature is not to be feared but rather embraced and understood, for it gives meaning to life. The expression of nature in Buddhism combines the concepts of reverence for life and nature as teacher. The stillness and flexibility of trees, the patience of insects, and the firmness of the earth are all qualities to be explored and internalized. The value of nonaction—the wisdom of silence and stillness—can best be learned from nature. Thich Nhat Hanh writes, "We should bow deeply and reverently before the monarch butterfly and the magnolia tree. The feeling of respect for all creatures will help us recognize the noblest nature in ourselves."[38]

Anthropocentrism, the central focus of traditional notions of development that aim to control and exploit the environment for the alleged benefit of humans, is at odds with Buddhism, especially its reverence for all life and its understanding of interdependence. Anthropocentrism places humans at the highest level of intelligence and understanding and sees other beings as less developed. It emphasizes the functional value of nature as food, fuel, and shelter and overlooks the profound truths found in nature.

Many of us in Southeast Asia understand the philosophy and spirituality of Buddhism as a mandate to work on behalf of all sentient beings. NGOs and religious communities have played a crucial role in this. Certain elders, such as Phra Sekhiyadhamma of Siam and Maha Ghosananda of Cambodia, have long been committed to social

anthropocentrism vs. holistic understanding

activism regarding nature. I am currently part of the Ariyavinaya project to transform the sangha. *Ariya vinaya*, or noble discipline, refers to the code of conduct and the significance of discipline in the lives of monks and nuns. More broadly, it is the connection between spiritual training and practical action. The Ariyavinaya project consists of a series of workshops that focus on how the Buddhist community can better meet the demands of structural violence and consumerism in society. The workshops emphasize the need for greater social engagement in monastic communities, an attention to gender issues in Buddhism, and alternative education.

The Forests

The Buddhist response to deforestation is a clear example of the tension between anthropocentrism and a holistic understanding of the web of life. Traditional Buddhist communities revolved around a forest monastery; the temple was the focus of political, spiritual, and educational life. Living in harmony with the forest was the reality. Once the process of industrialization began in Southeast Asia, however, forests became sources of fuel rather than sources of life. In Siam, the Royal Forest Department (RFD) promoted the destruction of forests in order to cultivate eucalyptus for the pulp and paper industries. First, the government ordered the destruction of thousands of hectares of forests and then, sensing the damage and the pressure from outside groups, the government ordered the protection of certain forests. Many of these newly protected areas were home to a number of indigenous groups and local people who had lived for generations in harmony with the forest but, under the protective legislation, could not maintain their livelihoods. The media characterized these people as "backward" and reckless in their use of natural resources; the government was presented as a savior and the local people depicted as the aggressors. A community forestry bill has been under discussion in the Thai legislature for several years. This bill, which lays out six classes of land, could help meet the needs of the indigenous people, but only if there is community participation. In Burma, the concept of community forests is used as propaganda in order to hasten the monoculture of eucalyptus. Governments cannot be the only source of decision making; it is imperative that local knowledge about sustainability be given primacy.

In August 2000, representatives of the Thai RFD stood by as lychee trees were destroyed as part of an upland/lowland conflict in Pa Klang Village over forest encroachment, water shortage, and chemical use. Pa Klang is largely populated by people from the Hmong ethnic group, and the systematic discrimination against them is representative of the treatment of many Hmong communities in northern Siam. Suradej Yangsaeng of Pa Klang Village believes that a resolution can be found only if responsibility is taken for the destruction of property by the lowland people, and if the government issues a clarification of the status of Hmong land. He says, "As the issue of our ethnicity is widely attacked and we are being blamed all the time, I would like to ask what the state wants the Hmong people to do. It seems there is no way out of this situation. Now I am very concerned about the people in our village. The lychee trees and their farms are their only livelihood."39 Yangsaeng also notes that the upland and lowland people rarely meet, and have wrongly depended on the government to act as a fair mediator for the conflict.

In Siam, government forest conservation has thus far been a series of halfhearted attempts to make up for past sins, mainly at the expense of communities and the livelihood of working people. Environmentalism, as advocated by the government, is a farce and must be replaced by a new understanding of the mutually dependent relationship between all forms of nature.

A renewed interest in Buddhist tree ordination ceremonies has helped to raise awareness about local ecology and celebrate nature. These ordination ceremonies are similar to forest robes ceremonies where laypeople present monks with clothes, food, and offerings for the temple. At a tree-ordination ceremony, the tree is sanctified by monastic robes and "the robes [stand] as a reminder that to harm or cut the tree—or any of the forest—[is] an act of demerit."40 These trees are important markers of the sacredness of nature, but education is necessary to connect this sacredness with the everyday patterns of consumption, waste disposal, and water pollution.

The Waters

In October 2000, the second public hearing for the million-dollar Thai-Malaysian pipeline and gas separation plan ended after less than an hour. The pipeline, a joint venture between the Petroleum Authority of Thailand (PTT) and Petronas, the national oil company of Malaysia, will run through forty-four fishing and farming villages in southern Siam. The hearing was ended after General Charan Kulavanijaya, chair of the public hearing committee, called for a vote on whether or not to proceed. But the only eligible voters were proponents of the project, who had paid one thousand baht each to attend. Police barricades had kept nearly five thousand protesters from rural areas from entering the building.[41] This type of mock participation orchestrated by the government is worse than no participation at all. It is demoralizing for organizers, and is part of a strategy of deflection and evasion practiced by the government with the aid of corporate powers. Over the past few years, many village leaders have been arrested and face criminal charges in court, a process that is quite exhausting. Nevertheless, they remain resolute in their commitment to nonviolent rallies, seminars, and protests to slow the PTT as they continue construction on the pipeline.

For the Future

Raising consciousness about preserving natural resources should start early, before they are threatened with destruction. Preventive measures such as education are part of the Buddhist environmental movement in Siam.

The Moo Ban Dek school in Kanchanaburi was established to provide poor children with a nurturing environment for the development of heart, mind, and will. The concept of education at the school extends beyond intellectual cultivation to the development of civic participation, environmental education, and spiritual understanding.

Students take responsibility for their self-government and self-discipline. Each day, time is set aside for doing chores, caring for animals, and swimming in the river. Nature at Moo Ban Dek is not separate from the school or the community, and environmental education is reinforced by science, civic education, and spirituality.

The annual Dhamma Walk is another way of spurring a change in the concept of nature and community. Initiated five years ago by Phra Sekhiyadhamma, a small network of socially engaged monks and NGOs in southern Siam, the Dhamma Walk continues to bring together a diverse group of participants. The walk was organized to bring attention to Songkhla Lake, Siam's largest lake, and organize a network in order to provide a greater local voice in policy making. The main issues concerning residents of the lake area were the depletion of fish, water pollution, reduced water levels, theft of water for urban and industrial uses, and loss of land.[42] The walk has been successful in starting a conversation about these issues, but with issues such as the pipeline looming in the near future, organizers of the walk are eager to find new approaches for effective change. A similar walk in northern Siam maintains the same commitment to forging relationships with local people, bearing witness to the effects of destruction, and advocating restoration at the walk sites.

Alternative communities are one way for people to regain control of local resources. The act of setting up a local currency system or a cooperative requires the participation of a large number of residents, and thus builds the social capital necessary to sustain any large-scale project. Alternative communities also transform economic relations by making consumers aware of the production cycle and encouraging economic transactions that are embedded in social life.

Small businesses committed to ethical environmental practices are at the base of the deep ecology movement. Finding practical alternatives to the current system is one of our biggest challenges. Although eco-consumption and eco-tourism can become warped representations of environmental ideals, they may be used as skillful means to help us achieve a critical mass of environmentally conscious people.

The movement to renew the relationship between humanity and all other forms of nature has had many successes and equally many defeats. Human-centered discourse is slowly changing, and there are many reasons for hope. Every time a tree is planted, every time a child swims in a river, every time we look upon each other with eyes of compassionate understanding, our commitment to interdependence is restored.

12. Buddhist Initiatives and
Peaceful Coexistence

THROUGHOUT FORTY YEARS of intense development and industrialization, Siam has witnessed increasing concentration of wealth in a handful of corporations at the cost of alarming environmental degradation, increasing poverty, and social disintegration. The rapid and expansive attempts to develop infrastructures, including the construction of roads and dams for better transportation and power generation, have resulted in the massive relocation of indigenous people. Through this process, they have lost pride in their cultural identity.

Export-led policies and the labor-intensive industries have uprooted local communities. The majority of Siamese farmers have been encouraged to shift from traditional farming practices based on self-reliance to the highly commercialized growing of cash crops such as sugar cane, cassava, and rice, all of which require the purchase of chemical fertilizers and pesticides. As a result, many farmers sink into debt; many farmers have lost their lands when they were unable to repay their creditors. Fluctuations in the world market have exacerbated their poverty. Often the children of indebted farmers are compelled to work in factories and businesses in urban areas to earn enough money to offset mounting debt service and the rising cost of living. Meanwhile the labor-intensive industries, in particular textile and electronic parts production and assembly, have been heavily subsidized by the state and have flourished in many urban industrial zones. Many landless farmers and their children have come to work in these factories. Their communal relationships are disrupted once they settle in industrial zones; the high cost of living has impoverished them further. But they have no choice. Even if they still have plots of land, their indebtedness and the uncertainty of prices perpetuates their suffering.

Worse, many of the workers in these factories have not been informed about, let alone protected from, occupational health hazards. Textile factory workers generally suffer from chronic lung problems due to the inhalation of cotton dust, and laborers in electronics factories suffer from the use of different chemical solvents. Worse, their employers often refuse to pay for their medical treatment, claiming that the illnesses have nothing to do with the dismal and hazardous working environment. Since effective measures to address occupational health problems have yet to be put in place, workers often receive no financial compensation for their deteriorating health and must bear the entire cost of treatment. And to contribute to the workers' woes, most physicians lack the moral courage to identify the causes of illness. Not infrequently, they detect a disease after it is too late for a cure. So the workers suffer from chronic health problems for the rest of their lives, and many die from these occupational health hazards. Understandably, they have organized themselves to demand proper compensation.

In 2002, an employee suffering from lung damage due to her work in a textile factory gave the annual lecture to the Komol Keemthong Foundation. She is leading a group of workers from all over Siam who are suffering from occupational health problems to demand due protection from their employers and the government. Speaking directly from her heart, she vividly elaborated how she, and the impoverished majority in Siam, have been exploited and impoverished, and how the existing social and political systems have not only failed to address their problems but actually compounded them.

If Buddhism can contribute to bringing peaceful coexistence to this tumultuous society, the following characteristics of Buddhist teachings will be most beneficial:

Buddhism encourages us to face suffering directly, not to avoid it. One of the most basic Buddhist teachings is the Four Noble Truths: *dukkha* (suffering), *samudaya* (the cause of the suffering), *nirodha* (the cessation of the suffering) and *magga* (ways toward the cessation of the suffering). By living with suffering and investigating it, we gradually understand its common characteristics. All suffering is believed to stem from the three main roots *(mula)*, namely, greed, hatred, and delusion. Many landless farmers and textile workers in Siam, for example, are not sidestepping their suffering. Instead, they contemplate it and attempt to find its causes. Doing so, they understand that it is not just they who are suffering. Their employers and the middle class are suffering as well. And because all are interrelated, a collective effort to solve the problem is needed.

Thus they gradually come to terms with the causes of their suffering: the unjust political, social, and cultural structures designed and implemented for the wealth of corporations. Inspired by Buddhist teachings, these debt-ridden farmers and heavily exploited workers— instead of blaming their suffering on specific individuals, such as factory owners or government officials—look for the causes of their suffering at the structural level, the basic understanding of which paves the way for the right solutions.

The solutions that they come up with are basically nonviolent. Understanding that their problems stem from economic development policies and structural violence (such as the cheap labor and the lack of workplace safety), they demand changes in the relevant structures, locally, regionally, nationally, and globally.

Thousands of these suffering poor—thrown off their land for dam and road development, evicted from forests cleared for eucalyptus plantations, suffering from health hazards at the workplace—got together in 1996 to form the Assembly of the Poor (AOP). They attribute their suffering to government policies and trade liberalization measures that favor corporations. They have been rallying patiently, sitting down and negotiating repeatedly with various concerned parties in the public and private sectors. Internationally, they work with groups such as the World Farmer Organization to find a collective solution to their problems. They are motivated by Buddhist teachings, which have been part of their traditional way of life. Buddhist elements are well reflected in the strategies they choose for their struggles.

They steadfastly hold to nonviolent principles. For this reason, I consider it one of the most remarkable social movements in the world. Yet government officials have been treating them harshly or even brutally. Their protest efforts include mass demonstrations, long marches, petitioning, and picketing, none of which involves violent measures.

With full knowledge that their problems are rooted in unjust political and social structures, they attempt to foster a wider understanding of their plight, in particular among the middle class. To achieve this, they have made peace with the mass media. In the beginning, news coverage of their movement was overly negative, and this resulted in public misunderstanding. Gradually they promoted a better understanding of the common sources of suffering among Thais. As a result, they have gained greater acceptance. Many in the middle class have assisted them through contributions or moral support. Some of them have joined the AOP in resisting social injustice and environmental degradation. A good example is a middle-class woman in Kanchanaburi Province who has led local human-rights and environmental groups to fight against the Thai-Burmese gas pipeline project.

Another important strategy they have relied on emphasizes the learning process. While protesting and demonstrating, with support from outside NGOs including the Spirit in Education Movement (SEM), these farmers and workers have developed reading materials, attended training workshops, and gone on study trips to better understand their problems at the structural level. They have also striven to identify solutions and to affirm their nonviolent practice. These learning processes are vital to the healthy growth of this movement.

Another example of these learning processes and nonviolent mobilization is illustrated by the evolving activities of the communities in Kudchum District, Yasodhorn Province, in northeastern Siam. After two decades of collective development and continuous effort, many projects have been concocted and implemented to address the causes of suffering such as poverty. Their efforts have enabled them to lead a self-sufficient way of life.

More than twenty years ago, realizing that they had to rely on goods bought from outside traders, they set up community cooperative shops in villages. This cut costs incurred from having middlemen. Then, supported by the district hospital, they were able to set up a fund to absorb the cost of pharmaceutical purchases. Later they found that although they had the money to buy them, the drugs were all either imported from the West or made with Western formulas. These medicines did not completely cure many illnesses and, worse, some villagers suffered all forms of side effects. When they realized their dependency on products and knowledge imported from the outside, they set out to find the real causes of their ill health and reach better solutions. They began to revive traditional medicinal practices including herbal remedies and massage. Eventually they became fully self-reliant in pharmaceutical production and consumption, and they began to sell their herbal medicines to people in larger neighboring towns.

However, they understood that any effective remedy also requires good preventive measures. They examined the food they consumed and realized the negative impacts of the heavy use of chemicals in their rice and vegetable plantations. Partly inspired by the visit of Masanobu Fukuoka, a natural farmer from Japan, they started to grow chemical-free rice and other foods initially for local consumption. Eventually, they thought about sharing the benefits of chemical-free rice with city folks, and found that they needed their own rice mill to do so. They set it up and are now enjoying increasing revenues from rice sales with better and guaranteed prices.

But greater profit is not the raison d'être of the rice mill. Through discussions, they came to understand that the main goal of their development project should be to enable local villagers to live self-sufficiently. To that end, they developed diverse products locally, including various kinds of foods and medicines. They conducted a workshop to analyze the flow of resources in their communities and found that despite their increasing income, their expenses were still high and many of them were still debt ridden.

For example, in Santisuk Village, which had thirty households, the expenditure on snacks alone was almost 100,000 baht per annum, which was equal to the expenditure on foods. Understanding the impact of consumerism, they realized they had to have more exchanges of local products in order to plug the leaks—that is, unnecessary payments to outsiders. After hearing about community currency experiments abroad, they initiated their own "Bia Kud Chum" in 1999. Distorted reporting and the narrow-mindedness of concerned government institutions (including the Bank of Thailand and the ministry of finance) made the use of Bia short-lived, however. The authorities claimed that the use of Bia would introduce instability into the national economy, a completely unfounded accusation. Japan, for example, has more than forty types of community currency in operation, and some of them have even been supported by local governments as well.[43] The same is true of many other countries in the North and South, including Canada, the United States, England, Argentina, Australia, China, Germany, and the Netherlands.

These locally interwoven and adapted development efforts have been springing up in all parts of Siam. Most of those driving these efforts have been inspired in some way by Buddhist, Islamic, or Christian teachings. I strongly believe that spiritual values provide a strong foundation for sustainable development initiatives. Through directly confronting suffering, one attempts to understand it and eventually seeks liberation—structurally, skillfully, and peacefully. In the end, this will lead to the peaceful coexistence of humankind and all sentient beings.

Culture and Change

13. From the Lotus Flower
to the Devil's Discus:
How Siam Became Thailand

I

THE MALAI SUTRA, a post-canonical Buddhist text composed by a Sinhalese monk, tells of the fate of those humans who commit wrongful acts in this life and therefore are reborn in a hell in their next life. In the hells they see beasts carrying lotus flowers above their heads. Seeing the beauty of the lotus flowers, they wish to imitate them. However, these beings do not realize that the lotus flowers they see are in reality discuses, which will sever and shred their bodies into pieces, causing excruciating suffering and torment. Because this story is known in Siam, Thai people may say that someone has "mistaken the devil's discus for the lotus flower." Such a person has *miccha ditthi*, or the wrong view, and sees goodness in something wrong or destructive.

In my opinion, the changing of our country's name from Siam to Thailand on June 24, 1939 was like mistaking a devil's discus for a lotus. In 1989, I proposed that Thai scholars get together and discuss the implications of the name change, but no one was interested.[44] In 1993, I suggested that an academic conference be held on the hundredth anniversary of Bangkok Era 112, a "turning point" in that historical period, but again there was little interest.[45] Four years later, there was a spate of special events and books on the reign of King Rama V. The Royal Thai Army even used the taxpayers' money to build a monument to the king in Sweden, allegedly to commemorate the hundredth anniversary of his first visit to Europe, when he initially lifted the discus of imperialism and colonialism above the head of his kingdom.

Although the Western powers did not formally colonize Siam, its people underwent internal or mental colonization, they were indoctrinated to mistake the devil's discus of foreign influence for a lotus. In fact, this process was set in motion even before the reign of King Rama IV, but it was King Rama V who made the danger real. He was reluctant to worship the discus unequivocally, however. Although he made many compromises with the imperial powers, he did so selectively. Meanwhile Burma and Vietnam were adamantly resisting the West. Thus they were colonized by the British and the French.

During the reign of King Rama V, we in Siam increasingly followed the ideas of *farangs* (Westerners), especially in terms of colonialism and absolutism. We did not foresee the importance of democracy. Nor did we know or care about the well-being of European citizens. In Bangkok Era 103, several individuals tried to act as the political and moral conscience of the king, but to no avail. Furthermore, the Thai ruling elites—the lords and masters—believed that one of the lessons learned from Bangkok Era 112 was to strengthen the country's military power, instead of dealing with problems gently and compassionately like a lotus flower rising from the water surface. Needless to say, military power was used primarily to crush or oppress the peoples of Siam— the Thai Noi, Thai Yai, Lao, other ethnic minorities, pro-democracy students, and so forth . This heinous conduct continued until 1992.

Toward the end of his reign, King Rama V repented and pointed to the danger of following the West's footsteps. The more the kingdom becomes Westernized, he suggested, the greater the threat. As King Rama III stated before his death, "Military conflicts along the Vietnamese and Burmese borders have ceased to exist. Only [the problem of] the Western side is left. Be wary of them. Do not fall prey to them. We should learn things that we deemed important from them. But do not respect or admire them unequivocally."[46] King Rama V conceded that it had been wrong to promote the construction of buildings using Western architecture, including the Chakri Palace, a building with "the head of a crown but the rear of a dragon." The palace, he declared, was not congruous with the kingdom's cosmological tradition, which links it to ancient India. On the contrary, he gave high praise to the royal palace in Mandalay, Burma; it was a superb manifestation of local and traditional architecture.

The King, therefore, wanted Prince Damrong to renovate and preserve the Bavorn Palace without its architectural structure being compromised. Damrong carried out this mission superbly. He ably supported the king's interest in preserving the country's heritage and tradition, which culminated in the establishment of a museum during the reign of King Rama VII. Unfortunately, the Bavorn Palace was stripped of most of its traditional architecture and beauty by the dictates of subsequent director generals of the Fine Arts Department, particularly after the country changed its name to Thailand.

The National Theater is now a symbol of supreme ugliness, a behemoth that almost completely blocks the view of the ordination (uposatha) hall of the Emerald Buddha temple. When Luang Wichit Watthakan was director general of the Fine Arts Department, he wrote and staged many extremely nationalistic plays that verged on fascism. Under him, the Fine Arts Department even controlled the kinds of dance dramas (rakorn chatri) that could be performed; these dance dramas had to follow specific story lines. This was because the Fine Art Department looked down upon the common people and local plays, perceiving them as inferior and therefore unsuitable for the national culture. In fact, the Thai word for culture, watthanatham, was a fairly recent construction, one that emerged simultaneously with the mongrel name "Thailand." Luang Wichit was the progenitor of this bastardized name. Prince Wan Waithayakon was his coordinator and the person who coined the word watthanatham.

To sum up, we maintained partial political sovereignty but lost our juridical and economic sovereignty since the reign of King Rama IV. By sending Thai students to study abroad and rapidly expanding the Western education system, we again discarded the lotus in favor of the discus. We must not forget that the lotus is the symbol of Buddhism. The lotus, no matter how lowly its origins, is able to rise and bloom above the water surface if it is not first eaten by turtles or fish—by *kilesa* (defilements). It relies on the threefold training: in higher morality, in higher spirituality, and in higher wisdom. Once the lotus rises above the water surface, water cannot saturate it, not even its petals.

Although the name "Siam" emerged officially only during the time of King Rama IV, Siamness was a tradition inherited from Ayutthaya and Sukhothai, from Sri Lanka and ancient India. Emulating the British empire, King Rama V devised a coat of arms, which displayed the vassal states of Laos and Malaya underneath Siam, the ruling state. In Bangkok Era 112, the French and British empires separated Laos and Malaya from Siam and colonized them. Until the kingdom became Thailand, Siamese rulers managed the tributary system using the emperor Asoka as a role model. Naturally, the Siamese kings assumed the status of the emperor. One of their main responsibilities was to ensure that the local rulers of Chiang Mai, Prae, Nan, Kedah, Kelantan, and elsewhere upheld Dhamma. For example, the Chiang Mai rulers granted ample freedom to the hilltribes people, enabling them to pursue their traditions and lifestyle as long as they maintained loyalty and obeisance to the court of Chiang Mai. In turn, the ruler of Chiang Mai was granted ample freedom as long as his court remained loyal to the king of Siam.

The king of Siam tolerated and promoted cultural and religious diversity in his tributaries. His tributary system included Vietnamese, Khmer, and Buddhist temples and Christian churches. Vietnamese, Chinese, and Mon monks received royal patronage. Wildlife and the lush jungles were protected. The duty of the Siam king is well captured by these Pali verses taken from the Book of Gradual Sayings:

> When kings are righteous, the ministers of kings are righteous. When ministers are righteous, brahmans and householders are also righteous. The townsfolk and villagers are righteous. This being so, the moon and sun go right in their course. This being so, constellations and stars do likewise;

days and nights, months and fortnights, seasons and years
go on their courses regularly; winds blow regularly and in
due season.... When crops ripen in due season, men who
live on these crops are long-lived, well-favored, strong and
free from sickness.

Admittedly, this idealism was not always upheld strictly. As the
kingdom was increasingly opened to foreign influence, the devil's discus inevitably and forcefully replaced the lotus. The worst blow was
struck when the farang education system eradicated the threefold
training of morality, spirituality, and wisdom. The new education system cultivated the brain at the expense of the heart. Without the wisdom of the heart to regulate, the smarter one is, the more dangerous
one can become. The more students go to study abroad and the longer
they stay there, the more they are enamored with farang culture. They
often end up knowing only about their respective areas of specializa-
tion, and hence their knowledge is compartmentalized. They cannot
appreciate the holism of life and mind, which must coexist in a dham-
mic relation with all nature. The Buddhist mode of education stresses
the nonattachment to self, nonharming of oneself and others, and
cultivation of inner peace, all leading to knowledge of one's real
nature. As human beings, we have different capabilities. If we use them
selflessly, wisdom will emerge to support all sentient beings and the
natural environment.

On the other hand, the farang education system is geared toward
augmenting selfishness, toward rising to the top of the socioeconomic
and political order by whatever means, even when it entails the abuse of
other humans, animals, or the environment. Farangs consider everything
as up for grabs—to be occupied, owned, conquered, controlled, or dom-
inated, whether for the sake of power, wealth, or self-aggrandizement.

Members of the Thai ruling class who were not educated abroad,
such as Prince Somdej Phramahasamanachao Krom Phya Vachirayan-
varorot, saw the flaws of farangs more perceptively than those who
went to study abroad. Nevertheless, he was both jealous and deeply

respectful of farang-educated individuals. Ultimately, his worldview began to change; he became more farang himself, especially in his attitude toward science. He even tried to scientize Buddhism, a highly unfortunate and deplorable act.

The devil's discus found its way into our house during the reign of King Rama IV and stayed on until the brief reign of King Rama VIII. It was on the whole a negative experience, for a while partially offset by the lotus rooted in Buddhism and the diverse and rich traditions of Siam.

On June 2, 1939, however, the devil's discus completely severed and supplanted the lotus. This was because the Thai ruling class looked up to farangs—even if they were Nazis or fascists. Buddhism, our lotus, was transformed into a ceremonial religion, was raised to the altar, and severed from any social, cultural, and political significance. And it had no impact on the lifestyle of the ruling elites. The ruling elites even wanted to create something like a Buddhist counterpart of the Vatican.

II

As previously noted, the name of this kingdom was Siam until 1939, when it was changed to Thailand. It then reverted to Siam in 1946. Two years after the *coup d'état* of 1947, it was again decreed that the country would be called Thailand, and it remains so officially. Ironically, the kingdom has since been ruled by one dictator after another with very brief liberal democratic intervals. The name Thailand signifies the crisis of traditional Siamese Buddhist values. Removing from the nation the name it has carried all its life is, in fact, the first step in the psychic dehumanization of its citizens, especially when its original name is replaced by a hybrid, Anglicized word. This new name also implies chauvinism and irredentism.

The country's name change in 1939 signified a cultural as well as a political revolution, although its magnitude was far less disruptive than the Cultural Revolution in China. Put differently, June 24, 1932 marked the beginning of democracy (i.e., constitutional monarchy), while June 24, 1939 officially heralded the advent of military dictatorship. Marshal

Phibunsongkram (hereafter Phibun) was the main force driving the establishment of autocracy in the kingdom. Luang Wichit and Prince Wan served as his right and left hands. The former was the brain behind the state policy of official nationalism, which emphasized the primacy of the Thai ethnicity in the region. With Luang Wichit's guidance, Marshal Phibun portrayed himself as the leader of all Thai people. Here "all" was farcically and conveniently formulated to mean domination over Burma, Vietnam, Cambodia, Laos, India, and (parts of) China. And from the outset, Marshal Phibun's rule was designed as a dictatorship in the style of Hitler, Mussolini, and Tojo. Prince Wan tailored Phibun's image and policies, making them acceptable to society at large. Prince Wan was also the progenitor of various keywords, planting farang terms in Thai social and political discourse. Some of these words and their officially sanctioned definitions are still dominant today, setting the outer limits to our intellectual independence or freedom.

It is unfortunate that no one has seriously attempted to demystify and deconstruct Prince Wan's linguistic constructions.[47] Marshal Phibun established a number of academic institutions that were supervised by the Royal Institute and the Fine Arts Department, and he relied on the Department of Advertisement (i.e., information) as his mouthpiece. All newspapers were under the iron fist of Phibun and the Department of Advertisement between 1939 and 1944.

In reality, Phibun wanted to be the Kemal Ataturk of *Muang Thai* (a name I prefer to "Thailand"). He felt that Ataturk's reforms, which, for example, weakened the grasp of Islam in Turkey, were progressive. In 1932, Phibun played a major role in the abolition of absolute monarchy in the country. And when Phya Manopakonnitithada (hereafter Mano) conspired with King Rama VII to resurrect absolute monarchy in the kingdom at about the same time as the eruption of the Bowaradej rebellion, Phibun was a leading figure who convinced Phya Pahonphonphayuhasena (hereafter Pahon) to launch a preemptive strike and consolidate the power of the People's Party. This forced Phya Mano into a lifelong exile in Penang. King Rama VII fled to spend the rest of his life in England. Phibun, however, granted amnesty to Prince

Bowaradej, who ultimately returned from Saigon to spend the remaining years of his life in the kingdom.

The successes of Phibun and his cohorts of young cadres earned them the epithet "Young Turks." The Young Turks eventually got rid of all the Old Turks such as Phya Song Suradej, Phya Srisitsongkram, and Phya Senasongkram. Young cadres who looked up to the Old Turks were also purged from the military. They were mostly exterminated.

So it was impossible for Phibun not to envision himself as the Thai Ataturk. Just as Kemal Ataturk created a new Turkey on the ruins of the Ottoman empire, Phibun saw his task as building a Thailand out of Siam. Luang Wichit even insisted that the name "Siam" was an invention of Rama IV, a weakling who opened the country to the British empire by granting London extraterritorial rights in the kingdom. This showed that Siam was inferior to the West, always following their footsteps. Furthermore, Luang Wichit argued that the traditions of Siam were outdated and the main sources of its weaknesses. For instance, he believed the inhabitants of Siam were half savage and extremely ignorant, and their behavior showed an acute shortage of politeness or courtesy. These factors prevented the kingdom from savoring the fruits of modernity, from being seen as an equal in the eyes of farangs. Hence, why not use Japan as the benchmark of modernity and Tokyo's autocracy as a model?

Phibun perceived the dominance of the emperor in Japan as a major shortcoming of the Japanese autocracy. He could not completely eradicate the remnants of absolute monarchy in his country because of the staunch opposition of his close friend Luang Aduldejarat, who had promised Chao Phya Pichayenyodhin to protect the monarchy. Luang Adul received support from Pridi Banomyong. Thus theoretically the political autocracy of Japan served as model for Phibun, but in practice the marshal emulated Mussolini. Il Duce allowed the continuation of the Italian monarchy but maintained that he was above the king. Likewise, Phibun emulated Hitler, who fanatically proclaimed the supremacy of the Aryan race in the world's racial hierarchy. Hitler transformed Jews into racial, political, and economic enemies, and demanded their extermination. Similarly, Phibun relied on the pseudoscience of Luang Wichit to assert and scientize the supremacy of the Thai people. Luang Wichit substituted the Chinese for the Jews; the Chinese were portrayed as the enemies of the Thai people. Although Phibun did not condemn the Chinese to death in concentration camps, he found various ways to break their wills and limbs. Nevertheless, he colluded with a number of Thai-Chinese to embezzle government funds, helping to set in motion the wheels of official corruption.

Phya Pahon was the only Old Turk whom the Young Turks admired and respected. As a result, they asked him to take a lead in preempting the conservative counterrevolution planned by the government of Phya Mano. Subsequently, Phya Pahon had to assume the premiership in 1933. But Phibun ultimately engineered the downfall of Phya Pahon as he had done to other leading figures such as Phya Song and Phya Devahastin. Phibun eventually became the premier in 1938.

In 1939, led by Pridi Banomyong, Siam successfully abrogated extraterritorial rights in the country; Pridi inherited the mission from Prince Devavongwaropakon and Prince Devavongwarothai. But Phibun, with utter disrespect for the two aristocrats, was quick to steal the limelight. He gave some credit to Pridi's skills at the negotiating table, but largely attributed the success to the high competence of his government. Phibun held a grandiose ceremony to observe the success of his government and declared June 24 of every year the national day. He built the Democracy Monument near a new bridge that crosses over Klong Banglumpoo, which was named Chalermwanchat (National Day Celebration) Bridge. Phibun also decreed that the word "Thai" be substituted for "Siam" in the national anthem. Ultimately, he imposed a complete ban on the use of the word "Siam." Thus the *Siam Nikorn* and *Siam Rasadorn* newspapers became the *Nikorn* and *Thai Rasadorn* newspapers, respectively. And the Siam Commercial Bank became the Thai Commercial Bank. Montri Tramote composed a song which won the national award. Phibun heavily promoted it. The song goes as follows:

The 24th of June is the most auspicious day
The first sign of our democratic constitution
Beginning our civilized democracy
Thus Thai citizens have the rights for freedom
We are all completely happy
Because our nation state now has complete sovereignty

As the song suggests, the kingdom had complete sovereignty due to the successful abrogation of extraterritorial rights in the country. But Phibun was still dissatisfied. He contended that complete sovereignty would be restored only when the territories "lost" in Bangkok Era 112 were returned to the kingdom. This was a root cause of the Franco-Thai border disputes and unwittingly paved the way for the Japanese occupation of the country.

Pridi tried to arrest the violent, irredentist trend. He insisted that the Thai government should rely on the International Court of Justice to help settle the disputes over the lost territories.[48] Pridi even produced and directed the film *The King of the White Elephant* to promote nonviolence—but to no avail. Phibun had crossed the Rubicon. As a result of the Indochina War, the kingdom regained Battambang, Siem Reap, Mongkolburi, Sisophon, and parts of Laos from France. But when we sided with Japan, we "recovered" Kengtung, which we had failed to do in our last attempt during the reign of King Rama IV. And toward the end of World War II, Japan returned Kedah, Kelantan, and several other Malayan states to Siam; these states were returned to the British after the war. But, strangely, Phibun did not ask Japan for the return of Megui and Sarin, both of which had been under Thai suzerainty longer than the other territories that we got back because of our alliance with Japan.

Phibun was not responsible for winning the kingdom's complete sovereignty. Rather he was responsible for regaining many of the territories that the kingdom had lost. He gave his protofascist regime credit for this success and contrasted it with the pathetic weakness and incompetence of democracy and absolute monarchy. It should be recalled, Phibun contended, that the name "Siam" received royal and official sanction during the reign of King Rama IV. It was then that we lost Cambodia as a vassal state. During the time of King Rama V, we lost many more territories. As Khun Chumnongpumiwet stated to a number of political prisoners in Bangkwang prison:

> When we look back at Siam we can see that it lost many territories. This is primarily because of the incompetence of statesmen in those times. They were dishonest and were selfish. They did not perform their task out of real love for the country. They were simply obsessed with their social status and position and indulged in immediate gratification such as having young wives to appease their sensual lust. Moreover, they did not uphold justice and the merit system, engaging in nepotism when it came to political appointments or bureaucratic promotions. They did not care about the troubles of others. Anyone who presented them with gifts would have a flying career. This was why we lost so many territories in the past.

Although Phibun did not win all of Cambodia back, he believed that his decision to ally with Japan, which helped the country to regain various lost territories, constituted a major success. Small wonder that he established himself as the Thai Mussolini or the Thai Hitler. He built the Victory Monument as a trophy boasting his military prowess and success. In reality, more than anything else, the monument is a symbol of defeat, a reflection of Phibun's hubris. He wanted to sever all links between the old Siam and the new Thailand such as absolute monarchy; he did not, however, get rid of the young monarch, King Rama VIII, who was studying abroad.

Phibun's leadership meant that the rights and freedom of Thai citizens were severely circumscribed, if not completely vaporized. Oddly enough, many citizens unequivocally agreed with Phibun's politics. The marshal declared illegal such acts as chewing betel nuts, squatting on a sidewalk, and wearing the traditional Thai *panung* (pants). Thai music was deprecated and deemed old-fashioned. Likewise, Thai medical treatment was stigmatized as antiquated.

The marshal affixed the farang word "land" to "Thai," implying that the country ought to be farang. Thai numerals were discarded and the Arabic numerals were adopted instead. Phibun perceived farangs as the embodiments of universalism (as opposed to regionalism). Hence farang music became international music. Local hospitals had to be reorganized along Western lines and Western medical treatment was the only kind of medical treatment sanctioned by the government. And so on.

The Thai people were indoctrinated by statism or state worship. Statism merely replaced the king worshipping of the absolute monarchy years. King worshipping was mandatory in royal and official circles during the reigns of King Rama V and King Rama VI. For most of the populace, however, it was a matter of choice. On the contrary, statism was robust and omnipresent. The people were forced to worship the national flag every morning and evening, a dictatorial practice that has continued to the present.

Statism compelled the Thai people to dress like farangs (bonnets, gloves, neckties, etc.) and to adopt their lifestyle. City folk had to import tables and chairs to adorn their houses even if they preferred to sit on the floor. Boathouses became extinct, especially along the canals of Thonburi. We all had to use forks and spoons—and have used them ever since. Adopting the Western practice, Thai first names were soon divided along gender lines. Names with Chinese, traditional Thai, or Arabic essence were arbitrarily changed. Thus a Lieutenant Somboon became a Lieutenant Chatichai. A Dr. Sudjai became Dr. Sud. A Ms. Samran became Ms. Suntaree. The last name Siaokasem became Sivaraksa. Wat Sam Jeen (Three Chinese Temple) became Wat Trimitta (Three Friends Temple).

Worse, the cultural constructions of the ruling elites straitjacketed the people's way of life. For example, this practice culminated in the establishment of the Committee on National Culture. The committee had an impossible mission: to derive essence from a mirage. As such, it was guided by a false consciousness. And the cultural constructions of the ruling elites reflected their political and economic power. The ruling elites' practice of dictating the "proper" way of life to other citizens eventually opened the way for consumerism and monoculturalism, a chronic malaise bedeviling contemporary Thai society as well as societies worldwide.

The battle between democracy and dictatorship (of both the left and the right) in Europe did not find its way into Siam. The sole exceptions seemed to be Pridi and some of his students and colleagues. Many students of the University of Morals and Political Science were dizzy with rabid nationalism. Thousands of them even paraded to show their support for Phibun's attempt to regain the lost territories from France. Ironically, the United States and democratic countries in Western Europe all supported right-wing dictatorships at that time. On the one hand, they feared the spread of communism, radicalism, and revolution. On the other hand, they distrusted the masses, assuming with hubris that the common people were too ignorant and immature to pursue a democratic form of governance. They could not perceive the threats posed by Nazism and fascism until it was too late.

Since the time of King Rama V, successive Thai leaders did not appreciate the importance of democracy. Even though absolute monarchy was toppled in 1932, very few individuals were devoted to the cultivation of meaningful democracy. These individuals performed various hit-and-run offensives against the military dictatorship of Phibun—with varying degrees of success. After World War II, the democratic forces in the country gained the upper hand vis-à-vis Phibun. In 1945, they removed him from the positions of prime minister and supreme commander of the armed forces. They abolished the name "Thailand," restored "Siam," and maintained the name "Prathet Thai." Once again, the people were allowed to chew betel nuts, wear traditional Thai dress, and so on. But these changes did not have lasting effects. The years of statism had largely torn the people from their traditions, and authoritarian culture had sunk deep roots in Thai society.

Democracy, which was continuously subjugated between 1932 and 1945, survived by and large because the University of Moral and

Political Science acted as one of its pillars. The university's grounds served as the headquarters of the Free Thai Movement to resist farang and Japanese dictatorship. When the war ended in 1945, King Ananda Mahidol returned to the country. A new constitution was promulgated in the following year. Democracy had an opportunity to plant its roots in the kingdom; it could have been a democracy more profound than the liberalism and capitalism of farangs. It could have been inspired and nurtured by dhamma and the sangha. The old guard, who deplored meaningful democracy, used the mysterious death of the young monarch as a pretext to get rid of Pridi and squash the democratic forces in the kingdom. The democratic forces were also linked to the independence movements in neighboring countries. The old guard succeeded in 1947 and reinstated Phibun as the premier.

It took roughly two years before the marshal could lay a solid foundation for his political future. He revived many aspects of governance under absolute monarchy to widen his political base. Japan during the Meiji era insisted that it was reviving the emperor system to replace the shogun system. In reality, Phibun was a shogun more than anything else—except for the fact that he was not born into the nobility. In 1949, he changed the country's name back to Thailand. His autocratic rule was less vicious and violent than in the first phase of his premiership. Nevertheless, he nudged the kingdom into the orbit of the Pax Americana, which arguably was more dangerous than the one Japan sought to create during World War II.[49] At first, the marshal merely wanted American military aid to stabilize and strengthen the Thai army, which was radically streamlined after the defeat in the war. Phibun's policy, however, led to Siam becoming a mere satellite orbiting the American empire. Washington soon exerted influence on the country's military and police as well as economy and politics. With the aid of the CIA one of Phibun's minions, Phya Suriyanon, even created a state within a state.

In short, Phibun and his minions, with the assistance of the United States, built up the Thai military (and destroyed the Navy) in such a way that it became a subordinate state. And the United States led the Thai leadership by the nose at every turn—the Korean War, the Vietnam War, and so on. There were U.S. military bases in the kingdom just as there were Japanese military bases in the country during World War II. By the time Phibun realized the terrible consequences of his policy it was too late. When he tried to steer the country away from the American orbit, key figures in the Thai military establishment, with the prodding and support of the United States and the palace, removed Phibun from power. Marshal Sarit was catapulted to the helm of power.

Sarit not only destroyed Phibun and Phao but also Thai identity and democracy in every conceivable way. At least Phibun allowed democracy to exist formally in the kingdom. And despite worshipping the West, he was still an adherent of Buddhism, however superficially. Aside from nefariously supporting Phao and latter Sarit, the United States also deviously used the term "development" to oppress and subjugate the Thai people. The Americans even convinced the Thai military dictatorship to forbid monks to teach about contentment, about satisfaction with whatever is one's own. The monkhood was drastically weakened and many monks believed in the state more than in dhamma.

Through their massive propaganda machine, the Americans indoctrinated the Thai people to believe in the virtue of money and technology—the crux of "development" and globalization. This message, which glorified greed, hatred, and delusion, was broadcast daily via the "free" mass media and could be found in the local folk songs and dances (mor lum) of northeast Siam. The people were afraid to speak the truth to power and to challenge transnational corporations (TNCs) and other worldly powers such as the World Bank, the IMF, and the WTO.

At present, the power of military authoritarianism has been greatly diluted. Our country seems to be increasingly democratic—at least formally. But the rule of and by the moneyed class has become dominant since 1973. And TNCs have increasing leverage on our ruling elites. Although the United States pulled its troops out of the country in 1974, American influence still remains unabated. Besides, we have to face China, which is more meddlesome and powerful than Japan was during World War II.

All these constitute the devil's discus which the ruling elites and people in the mainstream have mistaken for the lotus. Many Buddhist monks and practitioners do not understand the intricacies and complexities of the Western discus. Needless to say, *bhavana* (meditation) alone, which brings about critical reflection, humility, and simplicity, is insufficient to counter the power of foreign capital. *Sutamayapañña* (wisdom resulting from study) is also essential to understand the deep structures of the farang discus. This must be linked to the Four Noble Truths and the Law of Dependent Arising in the social and political dimensions.

14. The Last Word:
Remembering Pridi Banomyong

WHEN PRIDI BANOMYONG PASSED AWAY in May 1983, the members of the Thai parliament, an institution he founded, did not even give him a minute of silent homage. Pridi had devoted his life to further the cause of human dignity and the well-being of his country. The suffering he had to endure and the sacrifices he had to make were, by any standard, immense. He believed that the common people, no less than the rich and privileged, have the right to participate in governing the country and to take charge of their futures. Aside from introducing meaningful and participatory democracy to Siam, Pridi also played a pivotal role in resisting the attempts by the great powers to colonize Siam, either formally or informally. Thus judging from his contributions and credentials, Pridi was as significant as the other great Thai leaders or rulers such as King Taksin of Thonburi and King Naresuan of Ayutthaya. However, a major difference must be emphasized. Unlike the other great rulers in Thai history, Pridi was a commoner who did not aspire to reap personal glory; he simply wanted to serve the people, especially the oppressed and marginalized, and to protect the system of constitutional monarchy.

Making sure that the monarchy remains under the constitution is no small feat. There are always elements in the political, military, and business circles that opportunistically strive to venerate the monarchy, by blunting or preempting, in a knee-jerk fashion, any criticism of that institution. The limited power of the monarchy as prescribed by the constitution can be easily transmogrified into something absolute. This has now become a conspicuous trend ever since Pridi was illegally overthrown and the Siamese polity deviated from the concept of *santi pracha dhamma*—peace, democracy, and justice.

Now that we are commemorating the centennial anniversary of Pridi's birth, I hope the members of both chambers of parliament are sufficiently endowed with moral courage and intellectual capacity to grasp the importance of upholding the system of constitutional monarchy—in both form and substance. The democratic constitution should be the highest law of the land, guaranteeing equality, liberty, independence, and demanding and rewarding life experiences for all—including those seeking refuge in the kingdom. We must expect nothing less. Otherwise the monarchy will not be able to coexist peacefully and benignly with the Thai people, especially with the poor and unrepresented, and the monarchy will be sowing the seeds of its own destruction.

15. Art and Beauty:
An Ethical Perspective

WHAT IS THE MEANING OF ART AND BEAUTY? This is not simply a philosophical question for intellectuals to ponder. Art and beauty are matters of everyday life. They profoundly affect us all. How we interpret them has immense social, political, and economic ramifications.

Some have said that the actions of Prajak Petchasingh, a former monk who has played a crucial role in preserving the Dongyai Forest, and of those who have protested the construction of gas pipelines in Kanchanaburi Province are responsible for preserving and promoting beauty. They are trying to preserve natural beauty as well as expose the truth to the public.

On the other hand, many have praised the present king of Siam for his multifaceted artistic talent. For example, His Majesty's version of *The Story of Mahajanaka*, which is from the Tripitaka, is widely acclaimed as an artistic project with an objective of teaching people more about Buddhist wisdom. Such praises—however sincere—are expected. At times, however, I question how profoundly the king understands the meaning of art and beauty. Is he not the same person who has ordered the construction of huge dams that are responsible for environmental degradation and for uprooting many traditional communities? How necessary are these dams for our society and what aesthetic contributions do they make?

I

There are many different and even opposing conceptions of art and beauty. In her book *On Beauty and Being Just,* Elaine Scarry draws a connection between beauty, on the one hand, and morality and religion, on the other hand. Scarry contends that the moral dimension of beauty is weakening, if not disappearing. She argues that individuals who seek or bask in happiness and those who protect beauty are not necessarily beautiful—that is, ethically beautiful—persons. On the contrary, individuals who seek or protect the truth must know the distinction between right and wrong. They must be virtuous and just persons. She insists that although we might be able to behold the beautiful sky, we may not be able to see immaterial concepts such as justice or freedom. The sky is physical matter; justice is not. Beauty is reflected in physical matter. However, our visible environment may also reflect our commitment to our principles and to truth. For example, if we value justice we would not construct an art museum full of beautiful masterpieces in a location that would threaten the natural environment or disrupt the livelihoods of thousands of families. We should not violate our principles in the name of physical beauty. In sum, beauty and justice are interconnected.

In "Conjunctions and Disjunctions" by Octavio Paz, real beauty is depicted as something beyond the apparent world, beyond the temporary and the transient. He argues that if we look deeply at our faces, it will dawn upon us that they are no different from our buttocks; our buttocks are not aesthetically different from our faces. Paz's view is quite similar to Buddhist teachings.

Let us now turn to the thoughts of the eminently quotable Vaclav Havel. In a 1990 speech, Havel laments that although we know a lot more empirically about the universe and the natural environment than our ancestors did, we do not understand their essence or substance as well. In many respects, Havel continues, our lives have benefited substantially from advancements in technology. But at the same time, we feel at a loss. We do not know where to turn. We become increasingly estranged from our lives—from the meaning of living. With a heavy heart, Havel concludes that the postmodern world teeters dangerously close to a nihilism where everything is possible, where anything goes.

Almost seven decades ago, Kumaraswami pointed out the distinctive features of Indian and Chinese arts. He noted that Indian art mirrors the experience of community life and that art, like food, serves life. Indian art reflects the wants and needs of local communities. Discussing the long and rich tradition of Chinese art, Kumaraswami explained that Chinese artists do not emphasize novelty, uniqueness, or the unexpected. Although there were discernible changes in artistic output, the artists generally did not will them. So these changes provide invaluable glimpses into the changing way of life in a particular period and locality. Chinese art thus reflects the power of life and the shifting tastes of the people. In other words, tradition is alive. Tradition is not something that mummifies art; tradition is not a static model to be copied or emulated. In conclusion, Kumaraswami insisted that the Chinese have no such conception as art for art's sake because art is inseparable from life. Art is an expression not of the love of art but of the love of life.

In the West, people are taught that more is better; one should seek more of everything every day. In the East, we are taught from the cradle that we can constantly reduce our attachments or wants. In the West, the quality or quantity of personal gain and possessions marks the good life. In the East, the good life simply means successfully overcoming the attachment to gains and possessions. Lastly, in the West, most people near the end of their lives simply want to lead a carefree lifestyle unburdened by work or stress. In the East, we hope to have successfully extinguished all worldly attachments by the twilight of our lives, preparing ourselves for the next world.

II

Any visitor to Luang Prabang will be struck by its unassuming beauty. The royal palace is a single-storied building, humbly and harmoniously coexisting with the surrounding temples and natural environment. The French colonnades that were subsequently built are also unimposing. In fact, they even help enrich the beauty of Luang Prabang. The French seemed to have understood well the meaning of beauty. They also did a remarkable job in renovating Angkor Wat and Angkor Thom, enabling beauty and ancient glory to blend with the surrounding forests and hills.

The city of Chiang Mai was also once very beautiful. Its charm and beauty appreciably declined after it lost its autonomy and ceased to govern itself. The Chiang Mai rulers were important patrons of the arts and hence of goodness. As a result, the temple served as the symbol and center of beauty and goodness. Buddhists believe that beauty and goodness help pave the road toward the highest truth. Equally important, the rulers of Chiang Mai enabled their subjects, including ethnic minority groups, to express their artistic talents freely—to search for beauty according to their beliefs or faiths. In large part, this meant allowing their subjects to live according to their distinct hopes and traditions. Finally, the rulers of Chiang Mai, like those of Luang Prabang, were at the forefront of environmental preservation in their regions.

Against this backdrop, the hill peoples were able to live among the forests, mountains, and streams, upholding beauty and goodness as their standard of living. They had their own rich cultures and traditions. The rotational farming practices of the hill peoples never contributed to deforestation. Although they also hunted for food, the hill peoples never threatened wild animals and fish with extinction. They hunted for survival, not greed. In this context, they related harmoniously and beautifully with nature for hundreds of years. Of course, the hill peoples did fight among themselves. But they did not resort to violent arms that lead to disproportionate harm and immeasurable suffering.

Artistic beauty as expressed through music and dancing was not a monopoly of the northern kingdom of Chiang Mai. In the past, whenever a ruler or official representative from Bangkok visited Chiang Mai, the Northern ruler would dance to welcome and entertain his distinguished guest. The Southern guest would likewise dance along with the host as they entered the city together. Needless to say, it was an impressive spectacle.

When Prince Damrong Rajanubhap first visited Chiang Mai, he no longer knew how to dance along with his host. He had to send an envoy to do so for him. This was a sign that the sun of the old form of beauty was setting. During the reign of King Rama V, Siam began to incorporate the Western way of life into its social fabric.

Life in the countryside was also greatly and negatively impacted. The beauty and goodness of the traditional way of life faded. In the past, farmers often wove their own clothes, including the ones they wore to till the land. While they wove, others often sang or played musical instruments. Similarly, people often sang songs while tilling the land or harvesting the crops. They shared their harvest with neighbors and offered it to the monks. Beauty and goodness were interwoven with this lifestyle. Additionally, the people's way of life reflected the harmony between the seasons and traditions—between nature and human beings.

Buddhism has this saying: If a monarch upholds Dhamma, his officials will do likewise. The head of each household and the clerics will also uphold Dhamma—and so will all the citizens. When all the inhabitants of the society practice Dhamma, there will be equilibrium in nature. In other words, there is a connection between morality, beauty, and harmony in nature. Buddhism envisages moral conduct as the natural state of being, as natural as the cycles of nature.

Technology and modernity uproot and destroy the traditional way of living and the traditional conception of beauty and goodness. Ugliness is supplanting beauty. Goodness is dimming. The quest for truth is now skewed by falsity and injustice, guided by money and power. All this is done in the name of "being civilized" or Western civilization. Science and technology are said to provide the answer to every question. The fact that the latest science and technology may trample beauty and goodness is easily and conveniently discarded. For instance, self-reliance has immeasurably weakened, nature is raped and its diversity leveled, and millions of people are exploited in the name of progress.

III

What does being civilized mean? Rabindranath Tagore once said that the civilization or culture of Asia is derived from the jungle, whereas the civilization of the West has its roots in the city. The term "civilization" is often incorrectly defined as the culture and way of life during a particular period or in a particular part of the world. But civilization does not really refer to any type of society. "Civilization" originally referred to the city way of life; being civilized simply meant living like the city folks. Aristotle unabashedly declared that living in the city is the only way to develop oneself and cultivate beauty, goodness, and truth. He argued that an individual living in the forest would have no time to do so. The bulk of that person's time would be spent simply on survival— on finding food, maintaining sanitation, fending off bandits, etc. For Aristotle, the larger and more complex the city, the higher it is in the hierarchy of progress. Beauty, stability, political power, and technological superiority are indicators of progress and civilization. The Romans, even more so than the Greeks, emphasized political power and technology. This seemed to be the dominant trait of the culture of the Roman empire.

As mentioned earlier, my country began to uncritically absorb the Western conception of progress and civilization during the reign of King Rama V. As a result, the traditional way of life began to be seen as inferior—as the source of the country's backwardness. We looked down on our values and culture without really understanding their roots or virtues. For instance, the moral underpinnings of the *tribhumi,* or the Three Spheres, are belittled.

We tried to replace traditional visions of beauty with Western ones. This is dangerous. Perhaps the appeal of Western images remains the greatest threat confronting Siam. Of course, we have retained Buddhism; we have not adopted Christianity. But willfully accepting the Western notion of civilization is even more dangerous than converting to a spiritual system that is not rooted in our heritage.

Buddhism has become only a formality. It is no longer a living tradition. It no longer reflects the marriage of our lifestyle and the natural cycles and processes of our environment. For example, in a book of etiquette that was composed during the reign of King Rama V and was a required reading in many schools, the inhabitant of the city is portrayed as superior to the jungle dweller. This view is contrary to the traditional vision, which sees the jungle as the root of civilization.

In the past, those seeking mindfulness often went to the jungle. The life of forest monks, like the jungle itself, represented natural beauty and simplicity. Upholding celibacy and mindfulness, the forest monks lead a noble life. Wanting little for themselves, they give more to others than they receive. The way they sleep, eat, live, and dress is simple yet beautiful. Because they rely on mindfulness to conduct their lives beautifully and naturally, beauty merges with goodness. This beauty is also pure. And through further meditation and mindfulness, purity combines with peacefulness. At this point, if one's inner potentials are used to serve all sentient beings, one becomes literally enlightened.

The purity, peacefulness, and enlightenment of these forest monks contribute to their beautiful behavior and help make them exemplars of natural living, morality, artistic development, and health.

IV

Many of the royal palaces in this country are built according to the Western conception of beauty. For instance, it was believed that a marble palace is a reflection of civilization. However formidable and awe inspiring, these palaces look out of place. They represent the sad juxtaposition of Western architecture and Asian background. There is no real synthesis. These palaces do not reflect the living experience of the local community. There is no harmony with the natural setting. The same logic applies to the construction of the numerous high-rises and the heavy reliance on automobiles, which pollute the environment.

Between the reigns of King Rama V and King Rama VII, the ruling elite fed the populace with inaccurate and incomplete descriptions of the benefits of Western civilization. For the elite, progress meant being like the West; there was only one way to be civilized. As a consequence, Western ideas penetrated the kingdom's social fabric, influencing culture and art, modes of thinking, developmental strategies, and the legal and telecommunications systems. Most Thai students who went to study abroad were severed from their cultural roots, uncritically admiring the West. They no longer understood the essence of their nation's art and beauty and believed that the truth can be reached only through Western logic and sciences. To sum up, they ended up in the worst of all worlds, failing to understand both the West and their own roots. This problem has not abated. For instance, I wonder how much the present Harvard-educated minister of finance of Siam understands about beauty and natural harmony.

The Thai people were abruptly and radically uprooted from their cultural foundation during the dictatorship of Field Marshal Phibun-songkram. After the kingdom's name was changed from Siam to Thailand in 1939, the Thai people underwent a crash course in Westernization. Some changes were relatively superficial. As already noted, for instance, people were ordered to wear Western clothes and were prohibited from sitting on the sidewalk and chewing betel nuts. Worse, since 1947 and especially after 1957, a handful of families virtually held the Thai population as hostages. In the name of redeeming ideas like development and democracy, they kowtowed to Pax Americana and capitalism, setting in motion more cultural and social shock waves. Popular movements were also crushed, and the people were robbed of their power and rights. Political and economic power was heavily centralized in Bangkok. Bangkok opened its doors wide to allow free passage of American imperialism and all its transnational corporations. The modern mass media and infrastructure enabled the American corporations to spread their tentacles to other Thai provinces. People everywhere in Siam were thrown off balance and could not escape. The traditional conceptions of beauty and goodness, which include self-reliance, self-sufficiency, humility, and sharing, were transformed into vices or weaknesses.

Shopping malls proliferated uncontrollably in the kingdom, and they have replaced temples as the center of community life. The upper and middle classes indulge in consumerism, leading selfish and apathetic lives, greedily depleting the natural resources, and polluting the environment. In many respects, they are no longer human beings; they have turned into human havings. So far, higher education in Siam, as well as throughout the world, has been more successful in producing competent servants of power than responsible and compassionate human beings. Things are unlikely to change soon, since the center of power has shifted to the central bank, a rich men's club that acts as a gatekeeper for transnational corporations, the World Bank, the IMF, international banks, and so on.

If people lack inner beauty, goodness, moral courage, and an understanding of the structural causes of injustice at the local, national, and international levels, how can beauty be found in buildings, literature, sculptures, and paintings? We must learn to treat life like a work of art.

V

Despair will lead us nowhere. In fact, there are many good reasons not to despair. The initiatives undertaken by the Assembly of the Poor in Siam in its quest for beauty, truth, and goodness are inspirational and heartening. We have a lot to learn from them.

The Assembly is a sustained, nonviolent, and popular grassroots movement that first became visible in the mid-1990s, but it originated in the early 1980s. It is an amalgamation of seven distinct networks, representing almost every region in Siam and comprising more than half a million members. At the heart of the Assembly are urban and rural small-scale agriculturists and manual laborers. They form the absolute majority in the movement. In varying degrees, all of them have been hard hit by the mainstream developmental strategies and dominant conceptions of progress, beauty, and civilization. Worse, the government has shown callous disregard for their plight, cynically hoping that the will of these awakened souls would eventually smother.

Nongovernmental organizations, monks, environmentalists, responsible intellectuals, students, and some individuals from the business community are strengthening the sinews of the Assembly. Simply put, the movement is able to transcend class and regional divisions. Its members have come to care about, promote, and benefit from one another's well-being. The circle of the Assembly's kalyanamittas is also expanding. A living symbol of a participatory movement, the Assembly is organized from the bottom up. It calls for a comprehensive reevaluation of the mainstream conception of beauty and for rediscovering the virtues of our cultural roots.

Moreover, the Assembly has set up a university for its members. Based on local wisdom and culture and enriched with lessons on, for example, sustainability, conflict resolution, Buddhism, resource management, and networking, it is the kind of educational institution that seeks to preserve and foster pride in a simple and beautiful way of life. It is the kind of education that people need to lead a prosperous life— one that nourishes their hope, rewards their efforts, and helps minimize their exploitation and oppression.

In conclusion, if we can fathom the subtlety, appropriateness, and crux of traditional conceptions of beauty and incorporate this understanding into our nonviolent struggles for equality, justice, and environmental preservation, then we may begin to savor beauty and goodness and eventually open the door to the truth.

16. Who Are the Contemporary Thai Buddhists?

IN THE PAST, Buddhism was an important part of the daily life of the Thai people. Almost everyone was a Buddhist. In the home and the temple, Thais learned about and cultivated Buddhism. Many Buddhist activities brought together family members, neighbors, and other local residents. The temple was an important cultural, educational, spiritual, intellectual, and medical center. In short, the lives of the Thai people revolved around the temple.

Growing up in this Buddhist cultural and spiritual context, the Thai youth understood that *dana*, or generosity, was important and benefited everyone. And when they grew up in families that upheld moral discipline and training, they understood the virtue of the five precepts.

Some children who had Chinese fathers but Thai mothers might be influenced by Confucianism, helping them to have respect for the elders. They would learn the virtue of obedience and uphold honesty and loyalty. They might not have training in higher morality, higher mentality, and higher wisdom, but they would abstain from abusing or exploiting others. Conversely, they might passively accept the unjust social order such as the Siamese feudal system *(sakdina)*. If they rejected the status quo as unjust, their nonacceptance stayed, of course, within limits. Otherwise, the existing social structure would have crumbled due to challenges from below.

The more Buddhist or Thai their mothers were, the less Chinese the children would be. This is because Buddhism emphasizes generosity more than the accumulation of personal wealth. The early Chinese immigrants wanted wealth more than anything else; to them, generosity would begin once they were rich.

The more a family was embedded in the culture of Buddhism, the closer it would be to the temple and monks, and the greater its understanding of the value of humility, simplicity, tranquillity, and mindfulness. Self-reliance would be cherished over magic, superstitions, and technology. Moreover, if the people got to know good and wise monks, they would be able to develop spiritually. They would cultivate moral courage and wisdom.

Puey Ungphakorn, whose father was Chinese, is a good example. As he has stated, his Thai mother and maternal grandmother led him to perceive the value of Buddhism. Although he never flaunted his Buddhism, he was a truly respectable Buddhist layperson—despite the fact that he rarely operated within the framework of Buddhist orthodoxy.

Many highly respected Thai Buddhist monks had personal backgrounds similar to Puey's; they had Chinese fathers and Thai mothers. A few examples will suffice: Bhikkhu Buddhadasa, Bhikkhu Bhadaramuni, and Phra Dhammacetiya of Wat Thong Nopakun; Phra Sasanasobhana of Wat Rajapradit; Somdej Phra Vanaratta of Wat Mahadhatu; and Somdej Phra Buddhacariya of Wat Pathum-kongkha.

We must remember that in those days families would send their sons to be ordained as novices early on. Temples and Buddhism would lay the groundwork for the elementary education of young Thai males. If they disrobed after a few years, they would pursue secondary education at home—often vocational training in agrarian practices. The dhamma still played a role, however. Fish would be caught in moderation. Animals would be hunted in moderation. Nature would be respected. Animals were exploited but always within limits. Those who were strongly influenced by the dhamma would avoid pursuing wrong livelihoods; they would completely abstain from butchering and selling animals, and from producing and selling weapons, poisons, and so forth.

When the sons got older, they could be ordained as monks, which is equivalent to pursuing a college education. They would stay in the order for one to four years and occasionally longer. They would learn to nurture tranquillity, spirituality, and inner culture during this vital period. They would listen to sermons and discourse every night during the Buddhist Lent. After Lent, there would be many merit-making festivals, which would help engender wisdom in the participants.

In every temple there would be monks who could guide people in moral and mental training, which enabled them to cultivate wisdom in gradual stages through study, reflection, and practice. Those who had completed this college education were given the title of *pandit.* It is equivalent to obtaining a bachelor degree. If they had learned to read the scriptures in Pali, and passed the examination of Pali studies, they would be called *phra maha* (great monk). This is equivalent to obtaining a master's degree. If they steadfastly practiced meditation exercises and were able to teach vipassana practice, they would be called *achan* (teacher), even after they had disrobed. This is equivalent to obtaining a doctorate degree. Those who remained monks for the duration of their lives would be granted unofficial honorifics such as "venerable teacher," "abbot," or even *somdej* (the highest title for royalty, mobility, and monks in the state hierarchy). These monks might also be granted official titles.

In the past, young males, high born or low, would be ordained in the same temple. In some cases, after they had disrobed, lifelong personal bonds would be forged between the ruling elites and commoners, such as the friendship between Prince Asdang and Phya Adorndhani. Although women were not given the same opportunity to be ordained, they had many avenues to study the Buddha-dhamma. Some female devotees became established spiritual and religious teachers, training many monks and novices. Upasika Naeb Mahaniranon and K. Khaosuanluang (Upasika Kee) are good examples. The temple was the center of numerous spiritual and cultural activities throughout the year. Many major events in a person's life would revolve around Buddhism. Of course, tinges of animism, magic, and Brahmanism could be perceived, but Buddhism was always the primary religious practice. Being Thai was synonymous with being Buddhist.

The weight of Buddhism depended on how well Buddhism blended with the culture of the Thai people. Thais in the central region often denigrated the Buddhism of the Lao people, accusing them of being too animistic. Moreover, the Lao people seemed indifferent to the demeritorious activity of cultivating silkworms. Of course, Thais were more than glad to buy Lao silk. Both the Thai and Lao peoples saw nothing wrong with fishing as a livelihood, however—as long as it was not done in excess. For instance, fishing or the taking of life in general was prohibited on Shaving Day (the eve of a Buddhist holy day) and on holy days. And fish in a temple pond were spared; all life within the temple's compound was safe. (Sinhalese Buddhists, on the other hand, would completely abstain from fishing, leaving it to Christian and Muslim fishermen.)

Every Buddhist community shared the penchant for generosity. Monks, novices, worshippers, mendicants, savage animals, spirits, etc. were all supported and nurtured. As for mental culture as a way of making merit, Buddhist laypeople in general find this more difficult than generosity and morality. They consider bhavana to be more important for monks than laypeople, and monks in the forest tradition place greater emphasis on bhavana than urban monks, who are more concerned with studying the scriptures. Also, urban monks are more concerned with chanting or other *tiracchanavijja* such as producing holy water and fortune-telling. In the past, some temples even provided lessons in music, poetry, painting, and architecture.

Ever since Siam opened its doors to the Western powers, the Buddhist condition has gradually deteriorated. Our ruling elites were sent to study abroad instead of to the local temples. During the reign of King Rama V, the kingdom adopted the Western education system and built schools and universities. Hospitals, theaters, libraries, museums, and nursing homes were established, overshadowing and usurping the role of temples.

Relegating the temple to the backseat, the Thai government invested heavily in education so that young people would be more knowledgeable about worldly affairs than the monks were. (In the past, monks were knowledgeable about both worldly and spiritual affairs.) This new education system eventually spread to the major cities and towns of the kingdom. It was complemented by the expansion of the new administrative system, which was made possible by technological advancements. The central government used a new occultism based on the worship of modern technology to indoctrinate the people. The new education and administrative systems both indoctrinated people to accept the power of the state unequivocally. Soon people began to look down on their local customs and wisdom, and looked up to the city folk and ruling elites, who are enamored by Western science and technology.

When Prince Vajirayana took charge of organizing the curriculum of the sangha during the reign of King Rama V, he focused only on the study of the scriptures. He insisted that the knowledge obtained from the practice of contemplation and meditation could not be positively evaluated. Thus any ecclesiastical graduate of Pali studies underwent examination only in the farang way. As a result, the study of Buddhism focused on the development of the intellect and was devoid of spiritual training. How then could the student attain even a modicum of wisdom? Moreover, moral training was straitjacketed by formality and orthodoxy. Other forms of moral training were merely seen as inferior methods. For example, the Dhammayutika sect was looked upon condescendingly. The practice of insight development was seen as dulling the minds of monks, making them impervious to social issues, especially the process of modernization.

The Tripitaka contains a section on heavenly beings. It also refers to various planes of existence: the celestial realm, the evil realm, the human realm, the realm of demons, and so on. Unable to prove the existence of these realms empirically, contemporary Buddhists dismiss them as myths. The concepts of the next life, the previous life, and reincarnation have suffered a similar fate. This tension has been left unresolved since the time of King Rama V. Advocates of Western epistemology have tried to interrogate Buddhism trenchantly. On the other hand, those with narrow minds and vision have flaunted their supposedly superhuman power to experience and understand the other worlds.

If contemporary Buddhists read the scriptures within the framework of Western epistemology, Buddhism will be at best only an accessory, at worst an expendable luxury. But if they are able to cultivate mental training and study the Buddha's teachings, they will discern the well-expounded Dhamma of the Exalted One: imminent here-and-now, timeless, inviting one to come and see it, leading inward, and to be seen by the wise through direct experience.[50]

We must not forget that whether we are Buddhists depends on the extent we have studied and practiced the Buddha-dhamma. If we have not, we cannot say that we are Buddhists.

* * *

At this point, I would like to share my personal experiences. The middle class emerged in Siam during my father's generation. My father's two brothers both went to Christian schools. The older of my father's brothers had also been ordained and was married to a Chinese lady. It was the custom of the Thai-Chinese middle class during the time of King Rama V and VI to send their children to farang schools. Although my grandfather was from China, my grandmother was a Thai born in Siam. As a Thai, my grandmother was also Buddhist. Her Thainess left its mark on her sons.

Every morning, my grandmother would provide offerings to monks. My aunts carried on this practice until the extended family broke down in Thonburi. After World War II, my aunts no longer visited the temple on Buddhist holy days. But the housekeeper continued to do so. She would return from the temple with "merit" (blessings generated through good acts) for us. After the Buddhist Lent, we would go to listen to sermons and engage in various merit-making activities.

None of my family members was sent for schooling at the temple. We believed that studying in farang schools was much more prestigious. At that time, even if one had not completed secondary education from a farang school, one still had a good chance of finding work in a foreign company. Those of us who went to temples did so only to have our fortunes checked. Only the housekeeper went to the two temples near our house to listen to sermons.

It seems to me that the influence of Buddhism on Thai society began to wane during the time of my father's generation. Although my father was to some extent a virtuous man—he gave particular emphasis on alms and generosity—he probably inherited these virtues from his parents and respected relatives rather than learning about them from the temple.

Contemporary Thai Buddhists fall into two groups: those who are Buddhists out of necessity because of familial and social dictates, and those who question the value of Buddhism. The latter group is prone to ask, "Why be a Buddhist when upholding certain basic moral values is sufficient?" (Several decades ago they might have asked, "Why don't we turn to Marxism?")

I will begin with the first group, those who have been exposed to the Triple Gems—the Buddha, the Dhamma, and the Sangha—but have not sought refuge in them. They treat the precepts as commands and formalities. Some may provide alms on their birthdays or funerals only. Buddhist teachings and practices are not necessarily at the forefront of their minds.

Although some of them may gladly be ordained as novices during the summer vacation, the ordination itself is an elaborate and expensive festivity, a carnival. Some young men may be pressured to be ordained as monks to please their parents—or to make merit for the royal family—for a week or ten days. How much will they be able to learn within such a short period? Worse, how many temples really strictly uphold the Vinaya. In some temples, older monks will invite new monks to have dinner on the very first night after their ordination. Asked whether eating dinner constitutes an offense, the older monks would reply, "Not to worry, a confession tomorrow will solve everything." In other words, the monks' way of life is merely a theatrical performance. This is better than in some temples where monks do not even confess the offenses they have committed. Some temples do not even require the routine monastic duties, or allow monks to perform them perfunctorily without understanding their meaning or purpose.

Those who invite monks to conduct sermons, chanting, or religious ceremonies often offer them substantial basic necessities, including money. This is akin to hiring monks. Monks who accept invitations in exchange for material benefits lose their simplicity and humility. Of course, the more invitations the monks accept, the richer they become—and the less time they have for poor people. The higher the ecclesiastical title of a monk, the more he will associate with the rich and privileged, and the more he will be deluded by power, wealth, and status.

It is not uncommon for a monk's lodging to be equipped with a television set, VCR, air conditioner, and other amenities, including a soft, fluffy mattress. That a monk is alone in his lodging with a female is seen as nothing wrong. Fellow monks do not criticize one another's wrongdoing. Rather they conspire to shroud these offenses. Many quickly turn into fake, shameless monks. Elder monks holding ecclesiastical titles often compete by collecting fancy cars and climbing the ecclesiastical ladder. The richer a temple, the more ornate its architecture. It is now difficult to find a temple that has preserved its traditional architecture, which harmonized with nature. It is even more difficult to find a temple that is socially engaged with the surrounding communities, especially with the marginalized, the disabled, the youth.

So how should contemporary Buddhists react? Should they convert to other religions, a conspicuous trend in recent years?

After October 1973, many young people told me that Buddhism had an opportunity during twenty-five hundred years to prove itself capable of improving society. And for thirty years, the United States was given the opportunity to lead the country toward peace and prosperity—but to no avail. It was time, they contended, to raise the flags of Marxism and Maoism to return justice to society—even through violent means.

I responded that Buddhism has a subtle and noble way of eradicating structural violence and injustices with the aid of nonviolence. I told them that the word "sangha" is akin to "commune." A Buddhism that is overly compromised by magic, the *sakdina* system (thai feudal system), capitalism, and consumerism is not a noble discipline, not an *ariya vinaya* (appropriate teachings and discipline laid down by the Buddha to be appropriated in changing circumstances). If they understand the Buddha-dhamma they will be able to contain violence through ahimsa. They may be able to overcome the enemy within, which is far more difficult than defeating external enemies. If they are able to create inner peace, they will be less attached to the self and thus will dedicate themselves to the well-being of all sentient beings. They will be able to find kalyanamittas who cooperate with them to rehumanize and return justice to society.

Thirty or forty years ago the younger generation accused me of being too idealistic and romantic. We may appreciate idealism, and in every step of our lives we may be mindful and happy, but this must not become a way of evading suffering. Rather, we should confront and understand the causes of suffering. In so doing, we will be able to overcome them according to the Noble Eightfold Path.

* * *

In societies that had no Buddhist roots, Buddhists realized that the first step they had to take is mental development or meditation, that is, training the mind to be peaceful and unshaken by mainstream values and propaganda (e.g., attachments to materials, wealth, prestige). As a result, the number of meditation centers in such society depends on the size of the Buddhist community. Good spiritual leaders or meditation teachers will pave the way for moral training, in which one keeps one's actions and speech in a normal state and refrains from abusing oneself and others. If one's mind is able to achieve mindfulness, then one will understand that morality refers to the normal state of society. In other words, one must struggle against social injustice and structural violence.

Those who are in search of Buddhahood (i.e., being awakened from the domination of defilements) will be unable to find it in most monks

and mainstream institutions. But if they are avid readers and are determined to find goodness, beauty, and truthfulness, they may find it in
the works of leading Buddhists. The works of Bhikkhu Buddhadasa
comes first to mind. I also think of the works of the Dalai Lama,
Thich Nhat Hanh, and the Venerable P. A. Payutto. especially Payutto's
Buddha-dhamma.[51] Although these works will facilitate our study and
understanding of Buddhism, we must not neglect the task of meditation practice. Only through studying and meditation practices will we
cultivate morality, mindfulness, and wisdom.

If contemporary people understand the substance of morality, mindfulness, and wisdom, they will seek refuge in the Buddha and the
dhamma; they will perceive the Buddha as the wellspring of wisdom
and compassion. As such, they will have mindfulness, follow the
Buddha's footsteps, and be awakened from greed, hatred, and delusion.
They will transcend suffering and experience peace, clarity, and translu-
cence, and will be able to burn the flame of love without emitting the
smoke of jealousy, selfishness, and possessiveness.

Appreciations

Direk Jayanama

DIREK JAYANAMA WAS BORN on January 18, 1905, being the eldest son of Phya and Khunying Upaipipaksa. His father was a leading judge of the Supreme Court. Direk himself was called to the Bar in 1928 and joined the ministry of justice. After the bloodless revolution in 1932, which replaced the absolute monarchy with a constitutional monarchy, he served in many government posts: clerk to the cabinet, deputy foreign minister, foreign minister (three times), minister of finance, and deputy prime minister. As a diplomat, he was the ambassador to Japan, the Court of St. James's, the Federal Republic of Germany, and Finland. In the academic field, he was the first dean of the faculty of political science at Thammasat University, where he received his honorary doctorate. He also held the chair of diplomacy at Thammasat.

Prior to accepting the position of dean, the military government had illegally come to power through a *coup d'état* in 1947. Field Marshal Phibun, the new prime minister, had offered Direk a number of political positions—all of which he turned down. At the time of the coup he was an ambassador at the Royal Siamese Embassy in London. The coup government asked him to continue this role due to his exceptional skills in diplomacy; his success in renegotiating and erasing the unequal treaty signed with London was a testimony to his great competence. Direk ultimately stepped down from the position of ambassador to London because he was against military dictatorship and for democracy.

Direk cherished and believed in human dignity. It was an affront to his dignity to serve under a military dictatorship. He made it clear that the military dictatorship constituted a betrayal of the promise of democracy to the people.

But Direk trod a fine and cautious line. He did not want Field Marshal Phibun—the new prime minister—to suspect him of being an enemy. The two were friends and had known each other for a long time. Phibun respected Direk's talents and trusted him. And Direk survived through the post-*coup d'état* period in part because of this friendship. We must not forget that when Pridi Banomyong launched a failed coup in 1949 to force Phibun out of power, he proclaimed Direk (who had no foreknowledge of this) the new prime minister. Moreover, when the young King Rama VIII was found dead in his chamber, Direk was the minister in charge of the royal household affairs. Many had wanted him implicated in this "regicide." He survived both ordeals.

Also, Direk survived through the turbulent and dictatorial postwar years because the powers-that-be perceived him as weak and therefore non-threatening. He was always polite and well mannered. He was a Buddhist gentleman with ample moral courage and inner strength. Because of their own turpitude the powers-that-be did not appreciate, much less fathom, these qualities in Direk. He was a devout Buddhist. In his public lectures, his books, and indeed his own life, one can notice the influence of the Buddhadhamma all through. He was perhaps the only Siamese Ambassador who was elected vice president of the London Buddhist Society. During his tour in Japan, he tried hard and successfully to bring the two Schools of Buddhism into closer contact. And while serving his last post in Bonn, he traveled far and wide to propagate the dhamma to the German people. His observations of Buddhist activities abroad were always reported to his compatriots at home through his speeches and writings, for which he was well known.

In any case, Direk became an effective dean and a great professor at Thammasat University. Professorship was a role he loved and was good at. He opened a new program in diplomacy, which eventually expanded into International Relations, and wrote a series of books on the subject, which were widely acclaimed at the time. His magnum opus is *Siam and the Second World War*, a book that has been translated into the English and German languages. In this volume, Direk included a picture of Pridi Banomyong—a very subversive thing to do at the time. It was his subtle and diplomatic way of expressing dissent against the military dictatorship. Pridi was an important political figure in bringing democracy to the kingdom in the form of constitutional monarchy. Earlier, while he was representing the Thai government in London, Direk had issued a passport for Pridi to enable the latter to escape into exile via Singapore in 1947.

During the war when Phibun also assumed the position of foreign minister he asked Direk to be his deputy; Direk however was more experienced in diplomacy and had served as foreign minister before. During the war, Japan also wanted Direk to represent the Thai government in Tokyo. Tokyo suspected Direk of being anti-fascist and anti-Axis and of aiding the underground activities of the Free Thai Movement. Japanese leaders thus wanted to keep a close eye on him. At first, Direk declined to accept this role—a matter that infuriated Phibun. He ultimately and reluctantly accepted it, however. In Tokyo, he won the trust and respect of Japanese officials and bought a mansion that became the grounds of the Thai embassy and ambassador's residence in Tokyo.

When the Second World War ended and Phibun was (briefly) out of power, Pridi wanted Direk to be the new prime minister. Pridi, the head of the civilian wing of the Rasadorn Party, highly trusted Direk, and for good reasons. Direk was a true Buddhist gentleman—he valued simplicity, humility, and honesty. He had risked his life various times to serve the interest of his people. Many rightly consider Direk as Pridi's right hand. More importantly, Direk was well recognized by the United States and Britain. Direk refused, reasoning that since 1932 the premiership had passed only into the hands of members of the Rasadorn Party. He did not want the Rasadorn Party to have a monopoly over the premiership—to monopolize political power.

Therefore, he proposed that M.R. Seni Pramoj, a royal descent and leader of the Free Thai Movement in the United States, be the new prime minister, a suggestion Pridi accepted.

Direk did survive the postwar years, but he did not prosper financially like many others. In fact, a negative correlation exists between the political positions he held and his financial fortunes; the more influential he became politically, the more his bank account dwindled, the smaller his residence got, etc. He did not use his political influence to enrich himself and his family. Toward the end of his life he was also in great debt even though his wife came from a wealthy and royal family. But he was always rich in compassion and sympathy for others, and his wife always supported him; they were a role model couple. He was a good Buddhist in leading both his political and personal life. Direk was like a lotus, pure and simple. He had a wife whose mind was equally beautiful. She also deserves respect from society. We cannot forget their immeasurable contributions to our great country.

The Celebration of the 100th Anniversary of the Birth of Kulap Saipradit

March 31, 2005

The 32nd Session of the General Conference of UNESCO decided that UNESCO will coordinate the celebration of the 100th anniversary of the birth of Kulap Saipradit on March 31, 2005.

Kulap Saipradit was born on March 31, 1905. He was a highly respected thinker, writer, and journalist. His works covered wide-ranging areas, including literature, articles, and poems using both his real name and many pseudonyms, the most well known of which is "Sriburapha."

Kulap Saipradit started writing at the age of 17, while he was a senior high school student. Later, he became a full-fledged writer and journalist, writing on topics such as politics, religion, philosophy, social affairs, and academia. He was also instrumental in promoting independence, democracy, sovereignty, freedom, equality, peace, human rights, and justice in the society.

Kulap supported democracy both before and after the political changes in Siam in 1932, through the newspaper for which he was responsible. This led to much discrimination against him, including the closing down of the newspaper, the locking up of the newspaper's printing press, and ultimately his arrest.

Kulap was a supporter of peace, and was against wars, both the Second World War and the Korean War, and his anti-war sentiment led to him being imprisoned for almost five years. He was the founding chairman of the Press Association, and served as its secretary for many years, before taking up the position of the president of the Press Association of Thailand.

On the literature front, his most famous works include *Lae Pai Kang Nah* (Looking Forward), *Khang Lang Parb* (Behind the Painting), *Songkram Cheevit* (War of Life), *Jon Kwa Raw Ja Pob Kan Eak* (Till We Meet Again), and *Look Phu Chai* (Real Man), many of which have been selected as normal and extra-curriculum reading by the ministry of education. His works have also been translated into a number of foreign languages including English, Chinese, Japanese, Russian, and have been adapted for television and movies for a long time.

Kulap Saipradit passed away in Beijing on June 16, 1974, after 16 years of exile in China.

The "Sriburapha Foundation" was founded in 1987, and presently awards the "Sriburapha" Award to writers who have created works that are valuable to society and humanity. The Bangkok Metropolitan Authority has also named a road "Sriburapha" in honor of Kulap Saipradit, and has created a plaque of his handwriting praising peace, installed at the Suan Santiparb (Park of Peace), which was built to commemorate World Peace Day. [As president of the Sathirakoses Nagapradipa Foundation, I proposed Mr. Kulap's name to UNESCO via the Royal Thai Government and I am also a recipient of the Sriburapha award in 1994.]

The Reverend Prebendary John A. Rogers

(1934–1995)

His mother called him Robin, so he was known mostly by that name. He and I first met on the train to Lampeter where we would both spend the next few years studying. I started from Bourne-mouth. He joined the train at Newport in Monmouthshire, his birthplace, which is supposed to be faithful to both England and Wales.

Robin and I started our first term at St. David's College (SDC) in October 1954. We both had our rooms in the Old Building of the College. Most undergraduates could have their rooms only for a year. But since Robin was appointed a chapel clerk and I was appointed assistant librarian, we had our special privileges.

Lectures were given only in the morning. Afternoons were free. For most, afternoons were for playing cricket, hockey, football, and the like. Robin was good at hockey. Often he would go to play at other colleges, like Aberystwyth, Swansea, Cardiff, and Carmathen. After the games we would go to drink beer at the local pubs. We felt freer there than drinking around Lampeter, as it would cost us five guineas if the censor found us drinking.

If Robin was not practicing or playing hockey, he would accompany me on my afternoon walks around the countryside of Lampeter. It was, and still is, rural and beautiful.

We usually had tea in my room or his. I sometimes cooked rice and Siamese curry for him and for some other friends. Although I didn't have to attend Chapel I often did. This made the principal once say publicly to the other students, "Even the Buddhists go to Chapel. Why don't you blokes turn up, too?" In fact, the principal and his wife, Mrs. Betty Lloyd-Thomas, were very kind to me. And, of course, they had known Robin when the principal was the dean of Monmouth Cathedral.

In those days SDC was a small community, all male students. Clark Kerr was then president of the University of California (UC) with its many campuses (altogether UC must have had half a million staff and students). Kerr asked Lloyd-Thomas, "How many do you have at Lampeter?" When the reply was 130, including staff and students, Kerr said,

"You must be in paradise." Well, we did not think we were in paradise! The food was fairly awful and we had to write many essays (although lectures could easily be skipped).

Most of my fellow students were ordinands like Robin. After their B.A. degrees they usually went elsewhere for their seminary training. At Lampeter, the Bishop Burges Hall was attached to SDC as a seminary of Middle Churchmen. It was there that Robin decided to stay after his B.A. degree.

I believe I was the first Asian and non-Christian at SDC. However, all through our years at Lampeter Robin never felt funny about my being non-Christian, as did some of our contemporaries. Many of my other friends felt that they had to whisper anything about a Church scandal, or who would drop their heated arguments about Churchmanship as soon as I entered the Junior Common Room. Robin kept saying, "Sulak is one of us. Our Church has nothing to hide. It is quite weak right now. That's why we should join the Church and work for the benefit of all people—not only for Christians."

During vacations I was often invited to stay with friends, either at Bournemouth, Blackpool, or Anglesea in North Wales. Robin once told me he was so sorry that he could not invite me to stay with him because his house in Newport was too small and only his ailing mother lived there. I did spend one vacation in Newport, however, staying with Tony Miller's family. We three and a few others swotted (studied) together in the public library during the day and then would go to the local pubs at night. On weekends we would go sightseeing together or go rowing in the public park in Cardiff.

I knew Mrs. Rogers quite well. She had her eye on a young lady she felt was suitable for Robin: a good looking red-haired girl who was a frequent churchgoer. But Robin was in love with Marcia, who was very popular with all of us in our small circle. Indeed, she was a wonderful friend and partner for Robin.

When they married in Monmouth Cathedral I was teaching Thai at School of Oriental and African Studies, University of London. The BBC had asked me to do some broadcasting for them because the King and Queen of Siam were to make a State Visit to the United Kingdom; the BBC also asked me to hire a morning dress from Moss Brothers for the royal occasion. I turned up at Robin and Marcia's wedding in that attire, appropriate for an usher. But I really looked like a penguin!

I was lucky to visit Robin and Marcia everywhere: first, when he served as a curate in a Welsh parish; later when he was co-rector at Old Fort in the East End of London; and finally when he was the sole vicar of Hampton. Not only did I stay with the Rogers, but I always attended Divine Service. When my son, Chim, was being educated in England both Robin and Marcia invited him to stay at the Vicarage, offering him much friendship and hospitality. Their two daughters were also kind to Chim, and my wife and elder daughter also stayed at the Vicarage. Indeed, our two families remained on intimate terms. Robin and Marcia once came to stay with us in Bangkok and it was wonderful to take them up and down the country.

As prebendary of St. Paul's, Robin was required to preach once annually. He prepared his sermon seriously, as he always did for his Sunday service at his Parish Church. However, he told me that at St. Paul's he could preach for only seven minutes and that the pulpit was so high up that nobody listened to the sermon. He said people went to St. Paul's only as tourists or to listen to music!

Since Robin had a good soul and a good sense of humor, as well as a lot of modesty, people who did not know him well might think he was only a regular clergyman. Yet he cared immensely for the welfare of others and for social justice. It was very appropriate when he was appointed director of ordinands, for he understood the young. They, I believe, trusted him and felt the warmth of his unassuming personality as well as the depth of his spirituality. He was also in favor of women's ordination.

Among my Western friends, Robin was unique in that he could easily relax and was usually contented. He bore no ill will against those who wanted to harm him. He had no ambition nor any sense of competition. He preferred collaboration to competition and was non-violent. He was just like a Buddhist Bhikkhu in an Anglican collar and cassock, although he wore that clothing only in church.

When he became ill he bore it very well. I was privileged to see him twice in the hospital. Late last year I told him to remain well, as I would most likely be returning to England in January 1995. He smiled and said, "Worth living longer to see you again." And we did see each other again. He even took me out to the local pub across from Hampton Vicarage. Although he had to order beer without alcohol, we drank together. He was very concerned about the case of *lese majeste* trumped up against me at that time. And he lived long enough to know that I had been acquitted.

When the University of Wales at Lampeter made me an honorary fellow and the Lampeter Society elected me a vice president, Peter Allison kindly enlarged the group photograph of the year 1957, with Robin and me appearing together, and gave us each a copy. Marcia had it framed and hung in the Vicarage to welcome Robin when he returned home from the hospital in January 1995. He was so pleased with that old memory. He and I and Bob McCloy thought we would go together to the Lampeter reunion in the summer of 1995 or 1996. I had also thought I would return to see Robin and Marcia, as well as other friends in England on October 31, 1995; but the sad news came that Robin had passed away peacefully on September 19.

Unfortunately, I could neither see him alive on October 31 nor could I attend his funeral on September 27. To commemorate the memory of this most dear friend, I asked Buddhist monks to perform a ceremony to transfer merit to Robin Rogers. For me, he is still alive in another world beyond. In whichever heavenly abode he may be, may he be aware that his Buddhist friend will from now on be dedicating merit to him, will always think of him dearly, and will always feel grateful for his wonderful friendship. *Seeds of Peace, Vol. 12, No.1, Jan-Apr 1996, pp. 49–51*

Open Letter of Dediction to David W. Chappell

(1964-2004)

Dear David,

Our friendship dates from the summer of 1977, when I was exiled after a bloody coup in Bangkok in October 1976. Some American friends skillfully arranged for me to teach a spring semester at UC Berkeley and an autumn semester at Cornell. Bob Bobilin then invited me to give a series of lectures to celebrate the 70th anniversary of the University of Hawaii at Honolulu. This is where we first met.

I remember vividly when I made the remark that there was no room for violence in the teaching of the Buddha. And you pointed out gently and politely that in the Chinese Buddhist tradition, there was a sutra that stated that if a bodhisattva knew that a robber was going to kill 500 passengers on the ship, out of compassion, the bodhisattva should kill the robber and suffer the personal consequences of that karma. I appreciated your remark. After the lecture was over, you inquired about my return to Siam. But at that time I was not sure when I would be able to return home and my future was most uncertain. You then said that after you finished your work in Hawaii that you would be teaching at the University of Toronto. You asked me if I would accept to teach a semester at UT if invited. I said I would but thought that you were just being polite.

Then at Cornell before the end of the autumn semester, you telephoned me from Toronto saying that the Center for Religious Studies at UT would like me to be a professor there for one semester. Would I accept? Of course I was overjoyed. Despite the cold weather that my son, Chim, and I had to endure there, your friendship was so warm. Besides you introduced me to a number of Canadians who have become friends—Bruce Matthews, John Ralston Saul, and Adrienne Clarkson.

My teaching load in Toronto was light and I was a full professor with a bit of the English academic tradition of high tables, Latin grace, and gowns. At Berkeley and Cornell I was a visiting lecturer since I did not have a doctorate. Toward the end of the semester you organized a colloquium entitled "Multiple Loyalties: Buddhism and Christianity in Crisis" and I was asked to deliver a paper on "Buddhism and Society: Beyond the Present Horizons." Those taking part in the colloquium were Wilfred Cartwell Smith, Roger Hutchinson, Abe Masao, and Will Oxtoby.

After the semester you took me to give lectures at Smith College and Colgate University where I met new colleagues like Ty Unno and John Carter who have become dear friends. You also kindly edited the paper and lectures I delivered at Toronto and elsewhere as a book entitled *A Buddhist Vision for Renewing Society*, which, since its first publication in 1981, has had three editions. Writings from this volume, plus a few other pieces, were later compiled by Tom Ginsburg and Arnie Kotler of Parallax Press into *Seeds of Peace*, which became my best-seller in the U.S. and which has gone to many editions and has been translated to so many languages. In a way, dear David, you made my work known in North America.

After you left Toronto and returned to teach in the warmer Hawaiian clime, you again invited me to teach, this time as a Numata Visiting Professor. You were the first to invite me to take part in the Buddhist-Christian Conference on the Future of Humanity in Honolulu in 1980. This was the beginning of the Buddhist Christian Society, and ever since this meeting I have served as a permanent member of the Cobb-Abe dialogue, known officially as the Buddhist Christian Theological Encounter, hence I have made more Christian friends.

In Honolulu, you introduced me to many such as Aitken Roshi, Glenn Paige, George Simpson, Majid Tehranian, Johan Gultung, and Bishop Fujitani, all of whom have become my good friends.

You and I also expanded our encounter with Muslims, some have also become personal friends, like Abdurrahman Wahid, Chandra Muzzafar, and Anwar Ibrahim. Master Sing Tao has become a wonderful spiritual link in this encounter — not to mention Ruben and Maria Habito.

I greatly appreciate your serious support for the International Network of Engaged Buddhists. Although some may question your decision to join the Soka University in the U.S., instead of staying on at Honolulu, people who knew you could not help but admire your skillful means in maintaining your integrity with justice and compassion. Of course, Stella was so pleased to be back in the LA area.

You and I have traveled to many places together whether for the

Buddhist Christian dialogues, Buddhist Muslim dialogues, or the World Parliament of Religions. I often stayed at your home and you stayed at ours. Stella and Nin have become good friends. It was always good to have Stella with us, especially at our last stay together in Barcelona.

You and I have dreamed up and drafted quite a number of projects for the better future of our world, whether they be alternatives to consumerism, the Spirit in Education Movement, overcoming structural violence, or the Second Bandung Conference in April 2005. However, many of our dreams have not yet been realized, particularly the last one, which was initiated by Abdurrahman Wahid while he was President of Indonesia.

As an ordained minister in the United Church of Canada who has become a serious practitioner of the Dhamma, you were not hostile to Christianity. I remember once we held a Buddhist-Christian dialogue at Tsi Lai Temple near Los Angeles. It was Palm Sunday. When Hans Kung celebrated mass to commemorate Christ's last supper, he invited all his Buddhist friends to take bread and wine with him. Some American Buddhists refused to do so but you and I participated willingly. You even whispered to me that Hans Kung's approach made you feel that you could return to being a Christian but you doubted whether your church would accept such a liberal approach.

For my 70th birthday, you kindly edited essays in my honor entitled *Socially Engaged Spirituality,* which came out on time—27th March 2003. So many friends from all spiritual traditions contributed so much—not just praise for my work, but also proposals for action, a number of which you and I would have liked to do together.

Kumarian Press liked the book so much that they asked you to abridge it for sale in the U.S. You would have liked to do it for my 72nd birthday—the sixth cycle in our Siamese reckoning—but you were so overcommitted to your family, to Stella, to your students and your teaching as well as your concern for social justice with compassion locally and internationally.

I admired so much your sense of humor and your sense of service and dedication. Your bodhisattva path was really to serve all sentient beings. But for me personally, I value our friendship the most. We may have been friends for only 27 years in this life. But we may have been good friends in many past lives and I am sure that we shall be good friends again in future lives before we both liberate ourselves from the cycle of birth and death.

The Buddha said that the first sign of the rising sun is the light of dawn; likewise the Noble Eightfold Path is preceded by *kalayanamitta* (good friends). David, you were the best of my *kalayanamitta*. You were so generous to me and others—not only with material things, but with your time, your energy, your heart, and your wisdom. I owe you so much and I will try my best to be as good, as generous, and as selfless as you during the remainder of this life. Then I will soon join you in the next life, in order to practice our bodhisattva path together until we can really enter the gates of Nirvana.

Yours in Dhamma,
Sulak

P.S.

Dear David,
You may not appreciate me ending this epistle by paraphrasing Phaedo when he spoke of Socrates as being the wisest, the most broad-minded, and the best. For me, this phrase is true for you.

Acknowledgments

ARNOLD KOTLER OF PARALLAX PRESS in Berkeley, California was my first American publisher, who kindly produced two of my books in the United States: *Seeds of Peace: A Buddhist Vision for Renewing Society* in 1992 and *Loyalty Demands Dissent: Autobiography of a Socially Engaged Buddhist* in 1998. *Seeds of Peace* has become my best seller in the United States and has been translated into German, Italian, Dutch, Korean, Sinhalese, and Indonesian. Because Arnie has left the Press, he took the initiative to contact Wisdom Publications in Boston, which agreed to publish this book in time for my 72nd birthday—March 27, 2005—the sixth cycle anniversary in the Siamese tradition.

The first editor who collected and edited my various articles and lectures for this volume is S. Jayanama, editor of the *Seeds of Peace* journal which has appeared every four months since 1984. He was assisted by a number of friends who used to be on the editorial staff of that journal, especially Chris Walker, Sonali Chakravarti, David Reid, and Shreya Jani. All this was done in Bangkok.

In the Fall of 2002, I was invited to be a Eugene M. Lang Distinguished Visiting Professor at Swarthmore College, where I met Chris Wharton, a professional editor, who volunteered to edit the whole manuscript *gratis*. Professor Donald K. Swearer, the Charles and Harriet Cox McDowell Professor of Religion and Philosophy at Swarthmore College, kindly wrote the introduction to this volume as he had indeed been instrumental in getting me invited to the College. I am so happy that Don is now the director of the Institute for the Study of World Religions at Harvard University.

At the last stage of production, Blaine Johnson generously read the proofs and improved the style of my English, together with my editor at Wisdom Publications.

I am grateful to all the above individuals, as well as others who have been helping me either in inviting me to write or to speak as well as in supplying me with new ideas, alternative to the mainstream. I am also grateful to those who encouraged me in the field of socially engaged Buddhism, especially when I faced difficulty with the Thai authorities. Last, but not least, are my Thai assistants who deciphered my illegible handwriting, typed my writings, and entered them into the computer appropriately.

S.S.

Notes

Chapter 1, Buddhist Solutions to Global Conflict, was first presented as a Padmapani Lecture delivered at the India International Centre, November 13, 2001, at the invitation of Tibet House, New Delhi.

Chapter 2, A Buddhist Perspective on Nonviolence, is based on a speech given at the University of Melbourne, March 21, 2002.

Chapter 3, The Real Crisis in the Present World, is from a speech given at the Thailand Islamic Centre on October 20, 2001 and published in the *Bangkok Post* under the title "Pious Principles Be Damned" on November 24, 2001.

Chapter 4, Culture and Reconciliation, is based on a speech delivered at the Adelaide Festival of Ideas, July 12–15, 2001.

Chapter 5, The Value of Simplicity and Humility, was delivered at the Fourth Conference of the European Network of Buddhist-Christian Studies, May 2001, in Hoor, Sweden.

Chapter 6, A Simple Monk, was originally published in the *Rigpa Journal*, September 2000, pp. 24–26.

Chapter 7, The Virtuous Friends of Christianity and Buddhism, was presented to the Fourth Conference of the European Network of Buddhist-Christian Studies, May 2001, in Hoor, Sweden.

Chapter 8, A Very Simple Magic, is based on a talk given in Brisbane, Australia, in 2001.

Chapter 9, Compassion or Competition, was presented at the Social Venture Network Conference, December 5–7, 2000, in Chiang Mai, Siam.

Chapter 10, Blessings and Courage, was presented at the Millennium World Peace Summit of Religious and Spiritual Leaders held at the United Nations, New York, August 28–31, 2000.

Chapter 11, Buddhism and Environmentalism, was written with Sonali Chakravarti.

Chapter 12 is the translation of an article first written in Thai

Chapter 13, From the Lotus Flower to the Devil's Discus: How Siam Became Thailand, expanded from a lecture delivered at the Centre for Southeast Asian Studies, Monash University, 1989.

Chapter 14, The Last Word: Remembering Pridi Banomyong, was delivered to the Thai parliament on the occasion of the centennial of Pridi Banomyong's birth, May 11, 2000.

Chapter 15 is the translation of a lecture presented at Chiang Mai University.

Chapter 16, Who Are the Contemporary Thai Buddhists?, is based on a speech given at the opening of the Buddhadasa Library in Wat Prathum Kongka on November 17, 2001.

1. This Buddhist definition of nonviolence is based on Samdhong Rinpoche, "Buddhism and Non-violent Action," *Ordinary Mind: An Australian Buddhist Review*, no. 15 (winter 2001): pp. 14–18.

2. This story is taken from Chaiwat Satha-anand, "Three Prophets' Non-violent Actions," in The Frontiers of Nonviolence, ed. Chaiwat Satha-anand and Michael True (Centre for Global Nonviolence; Bangkok: Peace Information Centre, 1998).

3. Sulak Sivaraksa, "Sulak at Sharpham," unpublished transcript.

4. Dhammapada, vv. 1–2.

5. Sulak Sivaraksa, *A Buddhist Vision for Renewing Society* (Bangkok: Suksit Siam, 1994), pp. 263–264.

6. Dhammapada, v. 5.

7. Sulak Sivaraksa, "Buddhism and a Culture of Peace," in *Buddhist Peacework: Creating Cultures of Peace*, ed. David Chappell (Boston: Wisdom Publications, 1999), p. 44.

8. Ibid., p. 43.

9. Thich Nhat Hanh, "Ahimsa: The Path of Harmlessness," in *Buddhist Peacework: Creating Cultures of Peace,* ed. David Chappell (Boston: Wisdom Publications, 1999), p. 159.

10. See Sivaraksa, "Buddhism and a Culture of Peace," p. 45.

11. See Sivaraksa, "Culture and Reconciliation," speech at the Adelaide Festival of Ideas, July 2001.

12. See Bernie Glassman, *Bearing Witness: A Zen Master's Lessons in Making Peace* (New York: Bell Tower, 1998), p. 42.

13. Michael Nagler, "Peacemaking through Nonviolence," www.gmu.edu/academic/pcs/nagler.html.

14. His Holiness the Dalai Lama, *Ethics for the New Millenium* (New York: Riverhead Books, 1999), chap. 11.

15. Nagler, "Peacemaking through Nonviolence."

16. Ibid.

17. Paul Wehr, "The Citizen Intervenor," *Peace Review* 8, no. 4 (1996): pp 555–561, www.colorado.edu/conflict/citizen_intervenor.htm.

18. Samdhong, "Buddhism and Non-violent Action," pp. 14–18.

19. Thich Nhat Hanh, *For a Future to Be Possible: Commentaries on the Five Wonderful Precepts* (Berkeley: Parallax, 1993), p. 13.

20. Thich Nhat Hanh, *The Heart of the Buddha's Teaching: Transforming Suffering into Peace, Joy and Liberation.* (Berkeley: Parallax, 1998), p. 94.

21. Thich Nhat Hanh, *Interbeing: Fourteen Guidelines for Engaged Buddhism.* (Berkeley: Parallax, 1987), pp. 23–25.

22. Information about Gush Shalom is taken from www.rightlivelihood.se and www.gush-shalom.org.

23. Uri Avnery, speech on the acceptance of the Right Livelihood Award, Stockholm, December 7, 2001.

24. Nagler, "Peacemaking through nonviolence."

25. Ibid.

26. George Lakey, "How to develop peace teams—'the light bulb theory,'" www.nonviolentpeaceforce.org/articles/how_to_develop_peace_teams.htm.

27. All definitions and examples are taken from Lakey.

28. David Hartsough, speech at the conference on Peacemaking and International Insecurity in the twenty-first century, Asian Institute of Technology, Bangkok, February 11, 2002.

29. *International Socialist Review Issue* 20 (online edition), November –December 2001, "The war on terror: The other victims."

30. See Leslie Sklair, *The Transnational Capitalist Class* (Oxford: Blackwell, 2001).

31. John Ralston Saul, *The Doubter's Companion: A Dictionary of Aggressive Common Sense* (New York: Free Press, 1994).

32. The Noble Eightfold Path includes Right Understanding, Right Thought, Right Speech, Right Action, Right Livelihood, Right Effort, Right Mindfulness, and Right Concentration.

33. I have wrestled with this issue for decades. See, among other works, the relevant essays in Sulak Sivaraksa, *A Socially Engaged Buddhism* (Bangkok: Inter-religious Commission for Development, 1988); *Buddhist Vision for Renewing Society;* and *Global Healing: Essays and Interviews on Structural Violence, Social Development and Spiritual Transformation* (Bangkok: Inter-religious Commission for Development and Sathirakoses Nagapradipa Foundation, 1999).

34. For instance, see the essays in Wolfgang Sachs, ed., *The Developmental Dictionary* (New York: Zed Books, 1997).

35. Sklair, *Transnational Capitalist Class,* p. 218.

36. See Sulak Sivaraksa, "Buddhism and Society: Beyond the Present Horizons," in *Buddhist Vision for Renewing Society,* pp. 158–211.

37. Quoted in Stephanie Kaza and Kenneth Kraft, eds., *Dharma Rain* (Boston: Shambhala, 2000), pp. 29–30.

38. Thich Nhat Hanh, "The Sun My Heart," in *Engaged Buddhist Reader,* ed. Arnold Kotler (Berkeley: Parallax, 1996), p. 164.

39. Quoted in *Watershed: People's Forum on Ecology,* November 2000–February 2001, p. 47.

40. Susan M. Darlington, "Tree Ordination in Thailand," in Kaza and Kraft, *Dharma Rain,* p. 201.

41. *Watershed,* p. 9.

42. Santikaro Bhikkhu, "Dhamma Walk around Songkhla Lake," in Kaza and Kraft, *Dharma Rain,* p. 208.

43. See T. L. Yufuin, "Small Town Bartering: No Yen? No Problem!" *Times* (London), February 18, 2002, pp. 22–23.

44. Subsequently, I made the same proposal to David Chandler, an American historian who was residing and teaching in Australia. Receptive to my suggestion, Chandler organized a conference on this subject matter at the Centre for Southeast Asian Studies, Monash University. Craig Reynolds compiled and edited the papers that were delivered at the conference (Reynolds, ed., *National Identity and Its Defenders: Thailand*, 1939–89 [Victoria, Australia: Centre for Southeast Asian Studies, Monash University, 1991]).

45. Ror. Sor. is abbreviated from Ratarakosin Sok, or "Bangkok Era" (a term invented by King Rama V), which begins in the year Bangkok became the capital of Siam. Rama VI replaced this designation with "Buddhist Era," which begins 543 years before the Common Era. I gave a talk at Thammasat University on the hundreth anniversary of Ror. Sor. 112 (see Sulak Sivaraksa, *Satthawat haeng wikrit thang tang lok lae tang dhamma, ror. sor.112 lae sasanasapalok* (Bangkok: Komol Keemthong Foundation, 1993).

46. Chao Phya Thipakorawong, *Phra ratchapongsawadarn krung rattanakosin rachakarn ti see*, vol. 2 (Bangkok: Kuru Sabsa Press, 1961), p. 188.

47. I briefly touched on this issue in *The Power of Language: Whose Academic Institutions?* (Bangkok: Spirit in Education Movement, 1997).

48. In 1893, the French took Laos and part of Cambodia from Siam to be under its protectorate. But when France was occupied by Germany in the late 1930s, Pridi argued, it lost its legal claim to Laos and Cambodia. Hence it should hand those territories back to Siam since it took them illegally to begin with.

49. On this issue see Daniel Fineman, *A Special Relationship: The United States and Military Government in Thailand*, 1947–58 (Honolulu: University of Hawaii, 1997).

50. This is a translation of a Pali verse describing the Dhamma: *sanditthiko akaliko ehipassiko opanayiko paccattam veditabbo viññuhi*.

51. Phra Prayudh Payutto, *Buddhadhamma: Natural Laws and Values for Life* (Albany: SUNY Press, 2001).

International Network of Engaged Buddhists

THE INTERNATIONAL NETWORK OF ENGAGED BUDDHISTS (INEB), founded in 1987 by Ajarn Sulak Sivaraksa under the patronage of His Holiness the Dalai Lama, The Venerable Somdet Phra Maha Ghosananda, and The Venerable Thich Nhat Hanh, links together engaged Buddhists worldwide. INEB deals with alternative education and spiritual training, gender issues, human rights, ecology, alternative concepts of development, and activism. Although primarily a Buddhist network, INEB has interfaith elements as well.

For more information contact:

International Network of Engaged Buddhists
666 Charoen Nakorn Road,
Klong San, Bangkok 10600 Siam (Thailand)
Tel 662-860-2194 Fax 662-860-1277
Email: ineboffice@yahoo.com
Website: www.sulak-sivaraksa.org/network22.php

The Great Awakening

A Buddhist Social Theory
David R. Loy
320 pages, ISBN 0-86171-366-4, $16.95

The essential insight that Buddhism offers is that all our individual suffering arises from three and only three sources, known in Buddhism as the three poisons: greed, ill-will, and delusion. In *The Great Awakening*, scholar and teacher David Loy examines how these three poisons, embodied in society's institutions, lie at the root of all social maladies as well. The teachings of Buddhism present a way that the individual can counteract these to alleviate personal suffering, and in the *The Great Awakening* Loy boldly examines how these teachings can be applied to institutions and even whole cultures for the alleviation of suffering on a collective level.

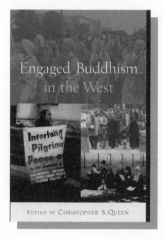

Engaged Buddhism in the West

Edited by Christopher S. Queen
560 pages, ISBN 0-86171-159-9, $24.95

"This is a deep and rich offering, an important look at the work of engaged Buddhists who have acted from their practice. The chapters in this volume show how engaged Buddhists are offering the fruits of their practice in very concrete ways in the West. These writers help us understand and gain inspiration from engaged Buddhism as it is practiced in daily life and in society today.'"
—Thich Nhat Hanh

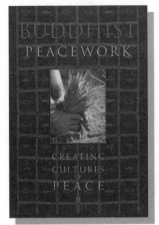

Buddhist Peacework

Creating Cultures of Peace
Edited by David. W. Chappell
256 pages, ISBN 0-86171-167-X, $14.95

Buddhism is known for bringing inner peace, but what about social harmony and environmental balance? We have a responsibility today to work directly with our own suffering and the suffering in our communities, the world, and the environment.

Buddhist Peacework collects—for the first time in one place—first-person descriptions of the ideas and work of eminent Buddhist leaders such as the Dalai Lama, Thich Nhat Hanh, Daisaku Ikeda, Robert Aitken, and others. These 18 essays explore the newest Buddhist social developments, the principles that guide Buddhist peacework, and the importance of ongoing inner peacework in developing a sense of kinship with all people.

The New Social Face of Buddhism

A Call to Action
Ken Jones ~ Foreword by Kenneth Kraft
320 pages, ISBN 0-86171-365-6, $16.95

"Jones's original *The Social Face of Buddhism*, published in 1989, came just in time to encourage many of us who were searching for the point were Buddhism and social action meet. The book was a beacon and we turned to it eagerly. Jones has now thoroughly re-written this work, as *The New Social Face of Buddhism*. We are lucky to have this new tool in our hands. The writing here is more fluid, and thus this volume is easier reading for an audience of Buddhists and fellow- travelers. We must do the socially engaged work that Jones writes about."—*Turning Wheel: The Journal of Socially Engaged Buddhism*

Wisdom Publications

WISDOM PUBLICATIONS, a nonprofit publisher, is dedicated to making available authentic Buddhist works for the benefit of all. We publish translations of the sutras and tantras, commentaries and teachings of past and contemporary Buddhist masters, and original works by the world's leading Buddhist scholars. We publish our titles with the appreciation of Buddhism as a living philosophy and with the special commitment to preserve and transmit important works from all the major Buddhist traditions.

To learn more about Wisdom, or to browse books online, visit our website at wisdompubs.org. You may request a copy of our mail-order catalog online or by writing to:

WISDOM PUBLICATIONS
199 Elm Street
Somerville, Massachusetts 02144 USA
Telephone: (617) 776-7416
Fax: (617) 776-7841
Email: info@wisdompubs.org
www.wisdompubs.org

The Wisdom Trust

As a nonprofit publisher, Wisdom is dedicated to the publication of fine Dharma books for the benefit of all sentient beings and dependent upon the kindness and generosity of sponsors in order to do so. If you would like to make a donation to Wisdom, please do so through our Somerville office. If you would like to sponsor the publication of a book, please write or email us at the address above.

Thank you.

Wisdom is a nonprofit, charitable 501(c)(3) organization affiliated with the Foundation for the Preservation of the Mahayana Tradition (FPMT).